BOLD AND BRAZEN

D1736128

BOLD AND BRAZEN

Exploring
Biblical
Prophets

BARBARA J. ESSEX

The Pilgrim Press
Cleveland

Dedication

With much love to the memory of my
friend and colleague at Pacific School of Religion,

DIANE THOMAS,

who dared to speak truth to power and whose life
was and continues to be the best example of what it
means to be bold and brazen

The Pilgrim Press, 700 Prospect Avenue, Cleveland, Ohio 44115
the pilgrim press.com
© 2010 by Barbara J. Essex

14   13   12   11   10   5   4   3   2   1

Library of Congress Cataloging-in-Publication Data

Essex, Barbara J. (Barbara Jean), 1951–
    Bold and brazen : exploring biblical prophets / Barbara J. Essex.
        p. cm.
    Includes bibliographical references (p.   ).
    ISBN 978-0-8298-1873-4
    1. Bible. O.T. Prophets—Textbooks.   I. Title.

BS1506.E88 2010
224'.007—dc22   2010022022

CONTENTS

ACKNOWLEDGMENTS

I am blessed to be surrounded by a great cloud of witnesses who continue to cheer me on. I am equally blessed to have family and friends who encourage and support me in this ministry of writing. I am grateful for the usual suspects—you know who you are!

I am grateful to Kim Martin Sadler, who always spurs me on with her support and tough love. I am grateful, also, for the support of all the folks at The Pilgrim Press who work hard to get my words out into the world.

And a special thank-you to members of congregations across this planet who wrestle with me to make sense of the Bible—your prayers make my work easier.

As always, any strength of this work is due to the constructive feedback of my conversation partners; all weaknesses are due to my own inadequacies.

PREFACE

old and Brazen: Exploring Biblical Prophets is about those strange characters of the Hebrew Bible called the prophets. These prophets have given us frameworks for understanding how to live under oppression, what it means to be the oppressor, and the meaning of social justice and peace. These personalities are responsible, in large part, for Israel's religious and theological understandings. Their oracles and proclamations form the basis for the development of Judaism. When Jesus engages the religious authorities of his day, he and they refer to "the Law and the Prophets" as authoritative sources for their work and understandings of the world. They are firmly grounded in the teachings of the Torah and in the teachings of the prophets who mediate between God and the people. Against the backdrop of the Israelite monarchy and later the super powers that dominate and control Israel, we hear the sometime strident voices of the prophets who dare to speak truth to power, to chastise a wounded and bewildered people, to offer hope when hope seems futile. So just who are these women and men who speak to monarchs and common folk? By what authority do they speak and to what end? To what lengths will they go to convey a message that they claim to be a word from God? These are some of the questions we will explore in this volume.

It is important to note that current biblical scholarship is moving away from the search for the historical personalities and more towards understanding the message of the prophets. We assume that the prophetic books are grounded in real personalities but we are not able to recover enough information to verify biographies of them. We try, then, to discern what their messages are and what issues their messages address. What we know with certainty is that their messages have stood the test of time and remain relevant for us today.

The prophetic literature of the Bible is divided into two groups. The Former Prophets fall under what we would call history and trace Israel's life from its entry into the promised land to the close of the united monarchy (the books of Joshua, Judges, 1 and 2 Samuel, and 1 and 2 Kings). The Latter Prophets begin with the longer books of the classical prophets (Isaiah, Jeremiah, Ezekiel) and end with the Twelve "Minor" Prophets (Hosea through Malachi). In this section, we also find the books of Lamentations and Daniel; they are not strictly prophetic works but contain prophetic elements. The Latter Prophets deal with Israel's life as a divided nation (Israel and Judah, or the northern and southern realms) and the collapse of each.

We are familiar with some prophets: Isaiah, Jeremiah, Ezekiel, Jonah, Amos, Micah, and maybe even Malachi. Others may be unfamiliar: Obadiah, Haggai, Nahum, Zephaniah. As with all volumes of this size and nature, we must make some decisions about what to highlight and what to leave for other volumes. Here, we want to look at some familiar passages from a few of the prophets and think more deeply about what they meant for ancient Israel and what they might mean for us.

Many denominations engage in ministries that focus on the common good. They want to embody the great command to love God and neighbor in contexts where there are gaps between the haves and the have-nots, the rich and the poor, the powerful and the powerless. And these churches turn to the prophets for help—for words, for frameworks, for God's voice in addressing the disparities all too prevalent in contemporary society.

The call for ministries that focus on social justice issues is a historical and ongoing one. Preachers often critique the status quo and are labeled as prophetic voices. Too often, though, there is little sense of what undergirds the prophetic work in the Bible. Therefore, the foundations for our work regarding critical issues and concerns are not sustainable over the long haul. This volume introduces the office, work, and motivation of "prophet" as we find them in the Bible to serve as a foundation for our ministries and mission both in the United States and around the globe.

We will take note that prophecy does not mean forecasting the future; prophecy is the attempt to make sense of a changed reality. For ancient Israel, the exile meant the end of life as it had been known. A people who had been promised land, identity, and community found themselves landless and dispersed throughout the known world. Instead of enjoying God's protection and prosperity, the people of Israel found themselves in foreign lands, trying to understand what had happened to them and why.

HOW TO USE THIS BOOK

Bold and Brazen: Exploring Biblical Prophets is a ten-week study of the Hebrew prophets for individuals and/or groups, designed to help us examine issues of mission, ministry, and social justice activism. One does not have to be a biblical scholar to study and understand the messages of these texts. The prophets are colorful and wonderful examples of God's work in the world. They are bold and brazen—verbal, audacious, assertive, and right on point in their messages. Our study should prove to be fun and challenging.

The book first offers background information and commentary about the prophetic office as we find it in the Bible. Then each Bible study unit includes a focus text; available background of the prophet; information about social, political, and theological contexts; suggestions for why the text continues to hold value for contemporary life; and reflection questions to help start a discussion about what we can learn from these characters and their stories.

Each study session needs about two hours; feel free, however, to make adjustments that work for you or your group. The materials you need include this book, a Bible version with which you are comfortable, and a notebook or journal in which to record your answers to the questions and your reflections on the lessons.

For group study, you may want to follow the suggested format:

- Assign readings ahead of time—the scripture as well as the unit to be studied.

- If necessary, set some "ground rules" for the discussion (for example, everyone will have an opportunity to voice his/her opinion without judgment from other group members; no one needs to agree with everyone else; no name calling; etc.).

- Begin each session with prayer, asking God for open minds and meaningful discussion.

- Review the information in the study unit; answer any questions.

- Use the reflection questions at the end of each unit to start the discussion.

- Share insights about the text, as much as people feel comfortable sharing.

- Assign the next unit.

- Close with prayer, thanking God for fruitful conversation and for God's help in preparing for the next session.

If you are using this resource for personal study, you should allot one and a half to two hours for each study unit. You will need a journal in which to record your reflections and questions.

At the end of this book, you will find a section with themes to consider for preaching and teaching about the prophets. The teaching section suggests ways to help persons enter the stories. The preaching section lifts up theological themes found in the stories. Finally, there is a resources section for those who wish to continue their study of biblical prophets. Of course, you should include any resources you find helpful to supplement the lessons here.

I hope you will find creative ways to make these studies fun and informative. There are no hard and fast rules about how to study these important persons in our biblical traditions. There is much we can learn from these biblical folks as well as about ourselves. I hope that these study units will help deepen your faith and broaden your service towards others. I hope you find this study to be informative, challenging, and inspirational. I pray God will bless you as you journey deeper into God's Word.

Introduction to the Hebrew Prophets

What do you think of when you hear the phrase "She is a prophet" or "His is a prophetic voice"? We sometimes think of persons who work against convention or who are troublemakers and rabble-rousers. Sometimes, we think of persons who seem able to predict the future or who see things "normal" folks do not see. We often throw the phrase around without really understanding what we mean. Almost anyone who critiques the status quo in politics is called a prophet. Those who call into question the way things are done and offer alternative perspectives are labeled prophetic. At least, this is the case when we are trying to be kind. Our assessment depends on who is on the receiving end of these so-called prophets' comments. If we agree with them, they are prophetic. We resonate with their message and critique; we sympathize or empathize with their perspectives. We cheer them on and find ways to support their causes.

If, however, we disagree with them, those who go against the grain are more annoying than prophetic. Their voices are loud, unreasonable, and irritating. If we don't understand their passion, we accuse them of overreacting or asking for too much. If their cause doesn't line up with our own self-interest, we shake our heads and dismiss them as narrow-minded, irrational, and too issue-focused. They represent special interests to the detriment of the common good. We deride them and find ways to subvert their presence and power.

What we will discover as we study the Hebrew prophets is that they are often on both sides of the fence—at times, the people listen to the prophets and heed their words; and other times, the people ridicule and even threaten them. The Bible itself offers an ambivalent picture of the prophets and prophecy; this ambivalence is evident throughout the ancient Near East. The problem is twofold: by what authority do the prophets speak, and how can we be sure the word is from God? These questions were asked not only by the Israelites but also by all those who were witnesses to the prophetic phenomenon. In some cases, the ambivalence is resolved because the words stand the test of time and their fulfillment is explicit. In other cases, the resolution doesn't come for decades or even centuries—only the perfect vision of hindsight bears witness to the validity of the prophetic word. In still other cases, the fulfillment of the prophecy remains to be seen. The inability to "prove" prophecy, however, did not stop it as a phenomenon.

Hebrew prophets continued to speak up and speak out about situations that put their communities in danger. Most of them felt they had no choice. They were compelled by God to speak—prophecy is God's doing and the prophets were instruments of God's will and bidding. And not all the prophets were happy about being called—Jeremiah and God went at it a lot because Jeremiah felt overwhelmed by the work God gave him to do. Jonah is portrayed as a self-interested reluctant prophet because he did not agree with God's actions. Despite the reluctance of some prophets, they all found ways to give in to God's call because it was always undergirded by God's presence and power. Without God's prodding and pushing, the prophets might have given in to the peer pressure to keep quiet and say nothing. But time and time again, the prophets declared not their words but the very words of God. It may be that modern-day prophets are motivated by the same call as those of ancient days.

THE PROPHETIC OFFICE

Prophecy, as a phenomenon, was fairly common throughout the ancient Near East—Israel did not "invent" it. Israel took a familiar occurrence and shaped it according to its own needs. Generally, each act of prophecy includes at least four components:

- A *divine being* who begins the process through words or by mystical means;

- A *message* to be given to a particular group of people;

- A *prophet* who delivers the message;

- An *audience* who receives the message.

Although prophecy was not uncommon, there was always some skepticism about the proclamation as well as some suspicion about the prophets. The ones receiving the utterances of the prophets often questioned the authority with which they spoke. Perhaps this is why most of the prophetic books begin with a clear declaration of God's call. But then the question arises—how can it be proven that the call is actually from God rather than something the prophet is making up? And therein lies the doubt—we can never be quite sure that any prophet has been called or that her proclamation is actually the word of God. God is not always helpful in making sure the integrity of the prophet is not questioned. When Moses seeks God's name, he is given the cryptic "I Am." When asked how he can be sure that his words will move Pharaoh to release the captive Hebrews, God basically says "you'll know when it happens." These are not necessarily words to stake one's life on. And that's the issue—the prophets do stake their lives on delivering God's word. They usually have some kind of experience with God, a theophany, which gives them the courage to do God's bidding. Experience and words . . . when these are grounded in God, one can be bold and brazen, no matter the outcome.

In the Hebrew Bible, prophets function in a couple of ways:

- Some seek to reform the society of which they are a member by chastising their contemporaries for not living up to the ethical and moral standards rooted in and shaped by the covenantal traditions of Moses and David.

- Others seek to make plain the political realities and the inevitable consequences of individual and corporate actions; these insights come from God rather than their own observations.

The prophets of the Hebrew Bible articulate where, when, why, and how God is at work in nature and in history. It is not clear why God calls the particular persons to the prophetic office; the texts show little evidence that these are necessarily persons who show great personal faith. There is no indication that the prophets' personal relationships with God are the reasons for God's revelation to them. Seemingly out of the blue, God takes their personalities and particular gifts into divine service. Each is sent to reveal God's working in a specific situation in Israel's life or to give directions to Israel at a particular time in history. Their messages, though, are so pertinent that they take on a timeless quality. Later prophets are able to take earlier oracles and pronouncements and shape them to fit more contemporary conditions and circumstances.

The prophets understand that the chief agent in prophecy is God and not they themselves. They are invested in the community to which they speak. Inevitably, their connectedness to community and the often inflammatory messages lead to tensions. Some of the prophets are persecuted (Jer. 20:2), some are killed (1 Kings 19:14), some are set against the whole land and the people (Jer. 1:18–19), and some are isolated (Jer. 15:17). However, the majority do not separate themselves from their people—the prophets consider themselves part of the whole community. They, too, stand under the indictment of God. God loves Israel despite its rebellious nature

and tendencies, and so do the prophets. For this reason, they inter-
cede before God for the life of the people. Some examples include
Moses (Exod. 32:11–14), Abraham (Gen. 20:17), Amos (Amos
7:2), Isaiah (Isa. 62:1), Jeremiah (Jer. 7:16), and Jesus of Nazareth
(Luke 23:34). The prophet stands in the gap caused by the rebellion
of the people against God; through prayer, teaching, love, and sacrifice, the prophets bridge the gap.

Biblical "judgment" is about divine justice—that is, God's intention for creation. God's judgment is over and against injustice
and serves a correcting function. Judgment is about bringing order
to unjust situations according to God's will and intention. God in-
vites humans—prophets, foreign monarchs and empires,
Israelites—to help bring justice, balance, and harmony back to situations that have become distorted or ignored. In the midst of God's
judgment, the prophets believe that God's intention for the future
can be hoped for and that it is given by God; however, when God's
intention is mocked or dismissed through arrogant practice and
policy, trouble (in the form of judgment) is sure to follow. Beyond
judgment, though, is God's intention for well-being, which embraces fertility, peace, justice, righteousness, and joy. Despite the
harshness of their oracles, the prophets also offer hope for God's
shalom (peace).

What we find, then, is that the prophets are clear that there is
hope for a good future that is rooted in Israel's ancient and honored
traditions, but only if leaders and people adhere to healthy and just
communal and social relationships as well as just and sound insti-
tutional practices and policies. They are convinced that God's purpose for the present grows out of God's old promises and commandments, which cannot ultimately be resisted. On the one hand,
the prophets deal with present-day life and what it means for the
community to live as people of God. At the same time, the prophets
deal with social pathologies and disorders that create injustice, pain,
and suffering. Community life with an eye always focused on justice

leads to both God's judgment and to God's mercy. The prophets are rooted in the past and are open to God's future; they believe that the present moment of life is critical because life-and-death decisions must be made that embody loyalty to God and that also shape public power and purpose.

THE PROPHETS IN ANCIENT ISRAEL

The "Latter Prophets" are grouped together in our Bible from Isaiah to Malachi, including the books of Lamentations and Daniel, and are named for the classical prophets of Israel. This section closes out the Hebrew Bible for Christians. Not all the prophets in the Bible are found in this section, however. Moses, Miriam, and Aaron are considered prophets; Abraham performs prophetic acts; Samuel, the last judge for Israel, is a prophet; Saul, the first monarch for Israel, joins a prophetic band shortly after being anointed; several women are designated as prophets, including Miriam, Deborah, and Huldah. The prophets are a diverse group of men and women who regularly speak about God's dealings with God's people. The primary task of the prophets is to ensure the people's fidelity to God and God's covenant with them. Their concerns include sincere worship, good stewardship, and harmony within the community characterized by acts of justice and compassion. And they speak as "insiders" who have a stake in what happens. They are not external objective observers; they are in community with the people with whom they communicate.

In the Hebrew Bible, the prophetic books are supplements to history. The prophets chastise monarchs and try to shape national policy by reminding leaders that God longs for justice and peace (shalom). Rather than predict the future (as the popular notion about prophecy goes), the prophets talk about possible outcomes if leaders and people forget their fundamental understanding of what it means to be people of God. By bringing keen theological insight to the issues of their day, the prophets can "see" into a future that brings destruction for their people. For the prophets, it's not rocket science—they and all the people have been taught from the very beginning that faithfulness to God brings prosperity and peace; unfaithfulness brings poverty and unrest. Throughout Israel's history, the nation often tastes the bitter fruit of their disobedience to God's will and way. These tastes are not the end, though, because God always sends leaders to help get the people back on track. The prophets, though, warn that one day God will lose patience and let the people live out the consequences of their actions. But they don't believe this—God has always taken care of them. Why would God ever stop doing that?

The prophets' role shifts when Israel is overwhelmed by more powerful nations. Instead of giving warnings about what may happen, they now try to make sense of Israel's changed social and political reality as well as their changed relationship to God. Instead of chastising, they now try to lead the people back to the moral foundations and obligations of their covenantal relationship. In the midst of devastating changes, the prophets remind the people that underneath God's anger, disappointment, and judgment are also God's assurance of salvation, redemption, and freedom. God is willing to give the people another chance, if they are truly repentant and willing to try again to live up to their covenantal responsibilities.

As we read the books of the prophets, we find that they often sound more like prosecutors than prophets. In fact, they are witnesses to God's "controversy" with or lawsuit against the people of Israel. As such, they rehearse God's long history with God's people in ways that take us back to the book of Deuteronomy and those books shaped by Deuteronomy. The prophets remind the people of God's steadfast love and point them back to covenantal obligations, responsibilities, and privileges. Furthermore, they bridge the transmission of the tradition of Moses to the present by outlining and interpreting their contemporary social and political realities and by calling the people to new religious consciousness—both ethical and spiritual—over against the popular notions of the day.

The prophetic books are firmly rooted in the teachings, affirmations, and convictions of the Torah. The covenant traditions of Abraham and Moses contribute to the dominant themes, patterns, and structures of prophetic proclamation. This contribution includes not only the saving tradition of the Exodus, which is reiterated by the prophets, but also the ethical tradition of God's commandments and the liturgical practice of covenant blessing and covenant curse. In addition, the Hebrew prophetic books are sometimes informed by the priestly traditions of ancient Israel, and their messages carry concerns about the reality of sin, guilt, right sacrifice, and the urgency of holiness. In some cases, the prophetic books reflect the wisdom tradition, which focuses on the disciplined examination of life's purpose and meaning. The prophets borrow images from the wisdom tradition as they state time and time again that all of creation is under the rule of God.

In other words, the prophetic books are rooted and grounded in older Israelite traditions. These works grow out of Israel's faith and life as people of God; the prophetic messages do not spring from some external source but rather from Israel's ongoing relationship with God, who is Creator, Redeemer, and Sustainer. Israel is to live as God's new community, a community that embodies justice as taught in the Torah and includes ethical, economic, political, and religious instructions for communal life.

The prophetic office in Israel arises partially in response to the people's request for a monarch. Initially, the establishment of the monarchy is a divinely ordained blessing. Israel needs a ruler so that it might remain on the land promised by God. But the monarchy is suspect from the start; while it has the potential to bring the ancient covenant blessings to fulfillment, it also has the potential to undo those same blessings. God is displaced as the sole sovereign over Israel when it wants to be like the other nations for military, sociopolitical, economic, and growth reasons and for national stability. However, despite misgivings, God gives the monarchy a chance. In fact, God establishes a covenant with David and grants him an eternal dynasty. That is, there is to be a descendant of David on the throne for all time. This covenantal understanding will be important for Israel's future and its relationship with God.

It is easy to judge from our twenty-first-century perspective that the request for a ruler is not a good one. However, for ancient Israel, there really isn't much choice. The conquest of the promised land is not going smoothly and, even after settling in the land, the Israelites constantly have to deal with bigger and stronger nations that want to conquer them. They need a monarch in order to stay solvent and to deal with the surrounding nations.

The Latter Prophets are a diverse group of men (and women) who regularly preach and teach from their own lives and experiences what God would have God's people do. These amazing persons refuse to be satisfied with the status quo and dare to voice their feelings about life under God's rule as it is distorted and subverted by leaders and the people. The prophets' job is to make sure the monarchs and people live up to their calling as God's own. When they fail to do so, the prophet calls them to repent and renew their pledge of allegiance to God.

The prophets also educate the people about how they are to respond to Israel's own growing imperialist tendencies as well as to the emerging superpowers of the day, including Egypt, Assyria, Babylonia, and Persia. At various times, each holds Israel in its imperialist grip. Under the reigns of David and Solomon, the united nation of Israel lives in relative peace with its neighbors. Not surprisingly, Israel itself becomes a superpower—both monarchs acquire territories and enjoy a lush life of luxuries; the military is able to keep the nation safe and keep subjected lands in order. But we learn that the union is tenuous even during the golden age of David's reign. As charismatic as David proves to be, he is not able to bring total unity to the nation. Tribal loyalties and sentiments are always just below the surface, waiting to erupt at any time. The tensions grow under Solomon's tenure—his ambitious building projects require extra taxes and labor commitments. The people bristle under Solomon's demands; we are told that Solomon loves "foreign women" as a symbol of his waning faithfulness to Israel's God. We can hear the grumblings and murmurs just below the surface and we anticipate some catastrophe just ahead. We know that the Deuteronomic tradition, which shapes the monarchical perspective, does not suffer wishy-washy faith; that Solomon accommodates the gods of his many wives and concubines can only lead to trouble.

Solomon's greatest achievement is the building of the Temple as a permanent place of worship—in fact, it is God's residence. The Temple is a magnificent structure and is dedicated with much fanfare and pageantry. After Solomon dies, though, the nation is divided:

- Israel, in the north, represents ten tribes (see 1 Kings 12–17), and the capital city is Samaria.
- Judah, in the south, represents two tribes, Judah and Benjamin, and the capital city is Jerusalem.

Each has a separate history filled with intrigue, mayhem, and ultimately despair. Each continues the tradition of prophetic speech and manifestations. As each nation goes through the changes that lead to their destruction, the prophets try their best to stave off elimination. Israel's wrestling with how to remain in the world, but not of it, meets its match in confrontations with Assyria, Babylon, and Persia. Israel falls first. The chaotic nation is overpowered by the Assyrians, who are seen as instruments of God's judgment against Israel for forsaking God and God's ways. Israel literally disappears.

Judah, more stable because of its Davidic monarchical foundation, is overtaken by the Babylonians nearly a century later; they have the benefit of processing the events that led to Israel's downfall. That is, they have time to prepare and to see if their fate might be different. History tells us that Judah's destiny mirrors that of Israel and it is not able to maintain its independence. The advantage of time, however, does afford the nation the opportunity to think ahead. What can they do to maintain their identity and hope even in the face of certain political death? This is the task the prophets fill. They dare to speak up about what the people must do in order to stay alive as an independent nation. When it becomes clear that Judah cannot hold off the superpower that is the Babylonians, the prophets help the people make sense of their reality. And what a tough job the prophets have. The fall of both Israel and Judah is interpreted as the judgment of YHWH.[1]

The prophets have to say tough things to leaders who have the power to grant life or sentence the prophet to death. Imagine having to tell your boss that she is doing the wrong thing for the wrong reason. Of course, the prophet's job is a little easier since his real boss is God (not the monarch)! But that doesn't always keep the prophet safe. The prophet's job description includes (a) explaining the massive disasters that befall the covenant people of God; (b) reminding the people of God's judgment and justice; and (c) leading the people back to the moral requirements of their covenant relationship.

True prophecy sometimes goes unfulfilled and this is discouraging even to the prophets (see Jer. 20:7 ff.). It is the word itself that must find a response in the heart open to God's invitation of grace. Much of prophecy has a messianic view. Ancient Israel has a history of looking for and expecting a savior and deliverer that starts in the time of Moses, continues through the period of the judges and finally rests in the monarchy. As each stage fades, the hope for a deliverer, a redeemer, a savior does not. And in its most trying times, the exile, the people's hunger for a savior intensifies.

Biblical tradition traces prophecy back to Moses. In the Pentateuch, the title of *nabi* is given to Moses, Aaron, Miriam, and

---

1. The God who reveals the divine identity to Moses is designated by YHWH, the tetragrammaton for the Hebrew name. English Bibles typically translate YHWH as "the LORD."

Deborah. The early function of the prophet is to stimulate patriotic and religious fervor. There are two Hebrew words translated "prophet" in the Bible: *nabi'im* (plural form) and *hozeh*. There are some differences, but scholars do not consider them to be major.

	Northern realm: ISRAEL	Southern realm: JUDAH
TITLE	nabi = "prophet"	hozeh = "visionary"
CAPITAL CITY	Samaria	Jerusalem
COVENANTAL FOUNDATIONS	Mosaic (Moses on Sinai) traditions	Davidic traditions
PRIMARY ROLE/TASK	Covenant spokesperson	Herald, representing the divine council
MODE OF COMMUNICATION	Word dominates	Both vision and word are dominant

God calls the prophet to interpret the divine will. God typically communicates through words, in dreams and visions, and through ecstatic or mystical experiences. The basic literary prophetic unit is a proclamation of judgment or salvation. Prophetic speech is given in the divine first person and introduced with the formulaic expression, "Thus says YHWH" or "The word of YHWH came to me." Prophecy is considered the very word of God. The books of the prophets are mostly written in poetic forms and categorized as oracles. There are prose sections in the books but poetry dominates. Poetry is a fitting genre because it uses symbolic language and powerful images to speak about excessive imperialism and oppressive leadership within Israel and among the other nations. Poetry allows the prophets to both castigate their oppressors and empower and inspire their own people.

Most prophetic proclamation highlights some aspect of the Torah ("law") and its communal demands. The prophets are like prosecutors in God's "lawsuit" or "controversy" against the people. The people fail to live up to their covenantal responsibilities and God takes them to court to determine the verdict against them. The prophets work for God to spur the people to repentance. The Torah is used to prove that the people have breached God's law. They turn away from and abandon God; they fail to embody the ethical instructions for community life as outlined in the Torah.

It would be nice if the books of the Bible were placed in chronological order; we could then read the books in order and have a better sense of the bigger story. But such is not the case. We cannot with absolute certainty date the books of the prophets; however, a rough chronological order of the prophets is: Amos, Hosea, "First" Isaiah, Micah, Nahum, Zephaniah, Habakkuk, Jeremiah, and Ezekiel. Judah, the southern realm of the divided monarchy, is where the Temple and David's everlasting dynasty are located. Amos is a prophet who continues the northern tradition of prophecy begun by Samuel and Elijah. There are many unnamed prophets (see Jer. 7:25, 11:7). The post-exilic prophets in rough chronological order are: "Second" and "Third" Isaiah, Haggai, Zechariah chapters 1–8, Malachi, Obadiah, Joel, and Zechariah chapters 9–11, 12–14.

Many people have issues with the Hebrew Bible. For them, God is too stern, too mean, too emotional. The God of the prophetic books is vengeful, cruel, and sadistic. These books are filled with horrifying images of God burning fields and striking men and women dead. It is difficult to understand why God is so bent on utterly destroying everything and even going so far as raising up enemies against Israel. While we cannot explain why the image of God is so violent, we can set this image in context.

The Deuteronomic, or D, tradition is one of several identifiable biblical traditions. Rooted in the law of Moses, D highlights the covenantal relationship between God and humanity. For the Deuteronomist, the main goal of Israel was to remain pure and uncontaminated by its neighbors. Every attempt was made to keep Israel holy and faithful to the one God, YHWH. The shapers of the tradition felt that any and all means were to be used to keep Israel true to its mission—to show other nations what it was like to live under God's reign. They felt that purity was the order of the day. The people of Israel were to place their utmost devotion in the one true God and to rely on that God for all of their needs and desires. By keeping the laws of Moses, the people were guaranteed prosperity and longevity. The D tradition shapes the treatment of the monarchy in Israel's story as well as the content of the prophets' message. This tradition calls the people to absolute and total allegiance to and faith in God. Israel experiences suffering and hardships because the people have turned away from God. Redemption and salvation are available only by turning back to God's covenant laws. The D tradition holds these beliefs because of the miraculous way in which the Hebrews were freed from Egyptian oppression— what a mighty God it was who had intervened on their behalf and brought them deliverance and liberation. Anything other than total reliance on God resulted in bad things. The impending doom that hung over Israel was twofold: that the nation would be separated from God forever and that the nation would be exiled from the land that God had promised.

War and violence are not praised in the Hebrew Bible; victories are seen as the work of God and God is praised. Israel's work was to settle into the land God had promised to them. They could not do so without going to war with the nations already occupying the land. Efforts at diplomacy were often frustrating and treaties were often broken.

For the people of Israel, God is a living, active force in history and in nature. God not only uses war and violence to the advantage of Israel, but also uses them to teach the people lessons. Israel is "punished" through the means of war and violence. Whenever Israel fails to win a war, it is because God has withdrawn divine power from the nation. War language and violent images are used to highlight God's judgment for or against Israel. When the nation turns away from God, it experiences defeat and oppression.

Despite the continual presence of and engagement in war and violence, the ideal state for Israel is not war but rather shalom—not just the absence of war, but the well-being of all people and all of creation. The word implies a wholeness that includes personal and communal well-being. Shalom covers a wide range of concerns: plentiful harvests, rest from war and fighting, safety from wild animals, health, contentment, and the presence of joy and righteousness (see Psa. 120:7).

The pictures of God that emerge in the prophetic literature leave us uneasy. We don't have to justify or make excuses for the God who engages in violent behaviors; the biblical writers are telling what they know to be true at the time of their writing. But war and violence do not comprise the entire story of God's dealings with humanity. While the biblical tradition is trying to convey the realities of its time, we are not to equate these words with God. A holistic perspective shows a God who grants free will to humans yet challenges them to exemplify justice and compassion in community. Thus, Israel is challenged by the prophets to care for widows and orphans, to show hospitality to the stranger, to treat each other fairly, to be compassionate to others as God has been compassionate to them, to treat all of creation with kindness, to take only what they need and not lapse into mindless consumerism and exploitation, to settle disputes with diplomacy. If Israel follows these guidelines for communal life, all will go well. If Israel does not, then the nation can expect to deal with consequences and repercussions.

We will find mirrored in the prophetic texts our own concerns about justice, community, the viability and purposes of political processes, the tension between self-interest and the common good. What many forget is that the prophetic books are meant to be over the top. The most devastating event in the life of ancient Israel has happened—the chosen people have been unchosen. Their fall from grace is not capricious or unfounded. Time and time again, God tries to woo Israel back into the fold when it strays. But nothing God does works. The nation continues to go its own way and to rely on its own resources. The prophets warn that one day God will have enough and will let them live on their own terms.

But we must not stop with the judgment of God. Judgment is not the only and certainly not the final word. The prophets remind the people, and us, that underneath God's anger, disappointment, and judgment are also God's assurance of salvation, redemption, and freedom.

EMPIRE AND TERRITORIAL EXPANSION

Biblical prophetic literature deals with national and international issues. The voices of the prophets speak to the people of Israel as well as to other the nations. The voices represent a response to the results of imperialism and domination. In fact, a number of biblical scholars, including Norman Gottwald and Walter Brueggemann, rightly state that ancient Israel came into being as an act of resistance to imperial forces. Abraham's call by God to leave his home and venture to another land is seen as God moving to resist the oppressive regimes of Mesopotamia. Likewise, the Exodus, which forms the center of Israel's theology and history, is further "proof" that God does not support empire in any form. The Hebrews are enslaved, exploited, and abused under the Egyptian regime. It is the cry of the people that captures God's attention and stirs up God's compassion. God delivers them from the oppressive imperial power of Egypt.

There is some dispute over whether we can rightly cite "imperialism" as the "enemy" in ancient Israel since "imperialism" is a modern term. In other words, can we apply a modern concept to ancient ways of being? We are constantly cautioned not to superimpose contemporary ideas and terminology on top of ancient systems; however, in this case, many scholars agree that the elements of imperialism were prevalent in the ancient Near East. Thus, we can talk about the Egyptian Empire, the Assyrian Empire, the Babylonian Empire, and the Persian Empire to highlight the military power and expansionist intentions of these nations.

The centerpiece of ancient Israel's history is the Exodus—the people are under the control of a superpower, Egypt, which extends its authority and power by acquiring territories beyond its borders and establishing economic and political control over them. Egypt displays the characteristics of "imperialism."

- First, it was a strong centralized state with aims to conquer other lands for a variety of reasons: to control trade routes; to take advantage of free labor; to take for their own use resources indigenous to the land being conquered; and, to shore up its military might by forming alliances in times of war.

- Second, it imposed taxes that its territorial holdings had to pay; these taxes were called tributes and all conquered lands were required to ante up.

- Third, Egypt's large landholders formed the nucleus of a ruling class that lived a luxurious life at the expense of those who did all the work. Laborers and domestic workers were paid low wages, if any at all. The workers did not have many options. For some, working for the state was a step up from their agrarian lifestyle, which depended on too many variable factors for success (good weather, good seed, good harvest, etc.).

- Fourth, rulers and those in power were equated with divine beings; some even considered themselves to be gods. So it was "normal" for pharaohs to demand the people to worship and honor them.

The price for imperial power was high—those at the bottom of the social ladder paid dearly in their labor, taxes, and time. Of course, those at the top had no problems with imperialism—they were the benefactors of the state-sanctioned oppression of others. The wealthy lived lives of great luxury and materialism.

A number of other nations display imperialist tendencies and are roundly chastised by the prophets for their deeds: Edom, Arabia, Sidon, Ephraim, Assyria, Babylon, Persia, and even Israel and Judah. None of the ancient nations are exempt—whether the other nations understand God's ethic of justice and righteousness is not clear. Ultimately, it doesn't matter because they all are accountable to God, who rules the universe. The prophets do not indicate that other nations should follow the Mosaic tradition, but the nations are to nevertheless maintain a standard of justice that ensures human rights and dignity for all people. The imperialist aim, though, is not about justice for all; rather, it is the accumulation of land, wealth, and power for a few while the masses work to support the state and its leaders. The motto might be, "only the strong survive" and "to the victor belong the spoils." In other words, there is no accountability for leaders who view imperialist aims and goals as the norm. Certainly nations with strong armies and advanced weaponry were able to implement their visions of an expanded state.

It is one thing for the "foreign nations" to indulge in practices that rob people of their dignity and livelihood. It is altogether another thing for Israel and Judah to engage in such practices. The Israelite monarchy proves beneficial on many levels: it ensures national security, allows Israel to expand its borders, and permits numerous military victories, which lead to greater wealth and prosperity for the nation. At the same time, Israel's newfound power causes it to lapse into idolatry and to accommodate the religious values and political practices of other nations. Rather than remain different from the other nations, Israel assimilates to its surroundings. The monarchs lead the way to apostasy and compromise. The monarchs allow their egos to sway them away from God; they give in to lust and greed, which leads to exploitation and abuse of the people God charges them to care for.

The transition from tribal league to state and empire greatly affects Israel—it changes the nation's religious, political, economic, and social understandings. Even when the nation splits into two realms, the people do not learn anything; they carry on as if they know what they are doing. They don't read the sign of the times; instead both nations allow "government" to displace God, and their monarchs use all too human means to achieve their goals. The prophets speak to human powers and they appeal to the people themselves. The prophets remind them that God does not condone any practices and policies that oppress the members of the human family, especially those most vulnerable—widows and orphans and strangers. The leaders in Israel and Judah are not to forget who they are—they are servants of God, God who loves justice and mercy, who is on the side of the poor and oppressed, who intervenes on the behalf of the powerless. Yet the monarchy does not deliver—and, in some ways, the monarchy hastens ancient Israel's demise.

God, though, continues to work in the life and history of Israel. God continues seeking those whom God has chosen. And when we get past the images of fire, brimstone, and destruction, we see God—waiting, listening, caring, and working to bring God's own back into the divine embrace.

THE CONTINUED NEED FOR PROPHETIC VOICES AND PRESENCE

Many of us do not like to equate the United States with empire or imperialism. As citizens of the "land of the free and home of the brave," we want to believe that our place in the world is a benevolent one. We want to believe that our country stands for democracy and peace. We want to believe that what we do as a nation is done out of a passion for freedom and a commitment to justice and compassion. We don't think twice when we hear the words, "USA—love it or leave it!" We find ways to justify our military presence in small underdeveloped countries around the globe with some seven hundred military bases in 130 countries (and perhaps thousands we don't know about)—we are there for their own good. We declare that we know what's best for others because we have the technology that makes a difference in the service of the common good. We even declare that it is God's will for us to help the rest of the world. In too many cases, the church condones the acts of government and may even encourage such acts.

It is important to remember that the modern equivalent of ancient Israel is not the United States and that U.S. citizens are not the covenant people of God. The notion of "manifest destiny" that gained a foothold in the nineteenth century was a policy of imperialistic expansion and territorialism; the propaganda set forth the idea that such expansion was (and continues to be) necessary and means to do good in the world. In other words, the doctrine states that the United States has the right and duty to expand its influence and power throughout the world and that such expansion is ordained by God. The history is long, sordid, and ambiguous. The United States has done good things both here and abroad; it has also has done great harm here and abroad.

We don't have to go back too far to find the embodiment of manifest destiny. The Pilgrims immigrated to North America seeking religious freedom and political autonomy. Many were farmers who had little education and little social status. Their faith enabled them to endure the arduous trip across the Atlantic and to reach the shores of their own "promised land." Indeed, their stories are peppered with biblical images and references. They saw their struggle to settle in the land as similar to that of the Hebrews settling in Canaan—including dealing with the people already on the land. The history that follows is strewn with courage and corruption, piety and destruction, faith and deceit; it is a mixed history of good and not-so-good deeds.

The early settlers were able to shake off the chains of the British Empire and at the same time destroy the land, culture, and lives of the indigenous peoples who had been living on these shores for centuries and who were now relegated to reservations. The colonists who established a government of the people, by the people, and for the people were also major players in the Atlantic slave trade that snatched some sixty million Africans from their homeland. The descendants of the early settlers celebrated liberty, justice, and the pursuit of happiness but exploited Chinese workers in order to build the Transcontinental Railroad. These same descendants established a strong-armed force and defense strategies during the world wars and at the same time interned its own citizens of Japanese ancestry in concentration camps, euphemistically called relocation centers. Tremendous advancements have been made in education and science, and yet syphilis experiments were conducted at Tuskegee Institute wherein nearly four hundred black men were infected with and not treated for the disease, in the name of "research."

The United States, light and beacon to the nations, paragon of freedom and justice, watchdog of the world, has a spotty domestic record and has been vastly unkind towards sectors of its citizens. And only through the rebellion of the people (both violent and nonviolent) and the use of legal strategies to hold the powers that be accountable has the nation been pushed to begin ending its oppressive and discriminatory practices.

Because our domestic affairs have been so uneven, we are not trusted on the international front. The "ugly American" is not hard to find; these are the "America, love it or leave it" folks. They are arrogant and refuse to learn about other cultures. They travel to other countries and rant and rave because "they" don't do things the way we do in America. That "America" is the name for the United States says something about who we are and how others see us; the United States is not the only country in the Americas—North, Central, and South. Our national sports teams are declared "world champions" when they only play other U.S. teams. Culturally and socially, we display an arrogance and privilege that alienates others and makes us feel superior. Our ways are different, not better.

U.S. foreign policy has been shaped by the sense of entitlement and privilege of a few. There is much rhetoric that covers the profit and power motives of our leaders. On the surface, leaders—political and corporate—speak as if their decisions focus on the common good. The leaders of this nation are quick to position themselves on other shores to make sure others are free; corporations quickly find opportunities to make money in foreign countries. Yet when the World Trade Centers were hit on September 11, 2001, the hue and cry of our citizens was, "Why do *they* hate us so much?" Unfortunately, our leaders and media did not help by educating our citizenry. Instead, we were bombarded with sound bites that generated fear and a desire to "get them back." Today, massive amounts of resources are funneled to "fight terrorism" so that there is very little for social services that are so needed by the poor and vulnerable in our nation.

The need for prophetic voices continues because we have not reached utopia. In places in this country and around the globe, people suffer greatly. The social ills of our world continue to grow despite advances designed to make life better. The prophets of ancient Israel did not have crystal balls to predict the future, but they understood the consequences of living life outside of God's purview. The values of community, peace, and compassion remain ideals to strive for. In a world where the rich still get richer and the poor are left to languish in despair and hopelessness, we need prophets who will stand up and speak truth to power. In a world where profits are placed over people, we need prophets who remind us of God's beloved community, where everyone has what is needed. In a world where might makes right, we need prophets who challenge us to beat swords into plowshares. In a world where U.S. policies and practices exploit others for money and power, we need prophets to hold us accountable for co-creating God's realm here on earth.

Many of us live comfortable lives. We have worked hard to achieve a level of success and comfort. And we are not likely to see ourselves as oppressors; most of us will declare we have no power—certainly, no power over others. We will declare, with pride, that we have pulled ourselves up by our own bootstraps and that others have the same opportunity. When we make such declarations, we subtly blame others for their own misfortunes—they need to work harder; they need to get an education; they need to speak "proper" English; they need to stop blaming others for their situation. These comments are unreflective and do not account for systems that are designed to create a gap between those who "make it" and those who do not.

Capitalism is not the same as democracy. By its very nature, capitalism creates social classes—some are well off and some are not; that's the way capitalism works. Capitalism determines who have good schools, good health care, good jobs—and who do not. It's no accident that masses of people struggle to make a living—they fuel the capitalist enterprise. Without the poor masses, capitalism doesn't work.

Democracy implies equal opportunity and advantages—at least, our understanding of it implies that everyone has a boot with a strap. In reality, the veneer of democracy has made us insensitive to the ways in which systems and structures shut out large numbers of people and how their participation in society is skewed. Racism and sexism are systems that have been the building blocks for democracy and capitalism. The list of "isms" is long and keeps numbers of persons from fully participating in society. The prophets challenge those of us who are comfortable to begin living from the perspective of those who are shut out of the process.

As long as humans think they know what's best, we will always need prophets to keep us humble. As long as we think our human institutions are altruistic and benign, we will always need prophets to keep us focused on God and God's ways. Until "justice roll[s] down like waters, and righteousness like an ever-flowing stream," we will always need prophets to remind us that God rules the earth and the heavens and we are always accountable to our Creator!

1

Whom Shall I Send?

READ:

Isaiah 6

FOCUS TEXT:

And I said: "Woe is me! I am lost, for I am a man
of unclean lips, and I live among a people of unclean lips; yet
my eyes have seen the [Sovereign], [YHWH] of hosts!"

(Isa. 6:5)

The book of Isaiah, the first of the classical prophets in the Tanakh and Christian Bible,[1] consists of sixty-six chapters and is a composite work of several different "authors" who lived in different historical periods. Scholars generally agree that the book is divided into three major parts:

---

1. Tanakh is the Jewish Scripture: T=Torah, N=*nebi'im* or prophets, K=*kethubi'im* or writings. The Christian Bible consists of the Hebrew Bible or Old Testament and the Christian Scripture or New Testament.

- Chapters 1–39 or "First Isaiah," believed to have been written by the eighth-century B.C.E.[2] prophet from Judah for whom the book is named.

- Chapters 40–55 or "Second Isaiah" (also Deutero-Isaiah), believed to have been written by an unknown prophet who lived in Babylon during the exile.

- Chapters 56–66 or "Third Isaiah" (also Trito-Isaiah), attributed to a prophet (or group of prophets) who lived in Judah after the return from Babylonian exile in 539 B.C.E.

The entire book depends on First Isaiah's message. First Isaiah prophesied to Judah and Jerusalem some time between 742 and 687 B.C.E. during the reigns of four Judean monarchs: Uzziah, Jotham, Ahaz, and Hezekiah. During this period, Judah had to deal with Assyria, one of the superpowers of the day. The book of Isaiah is rooted in the traditions of Moses and David—God is the great monarch of Israel and David is God's servant ruler; Jerusalem (Zion) is God's royal dwelling; and monarchs of the Davidic line are God's servants on earth. Isaiah shows that social injustice is evidence that Israel's relationship to God is shaky. Since the people fail to live up to their covenant and communal values, they will be subject to superior military and imperialist powers. Isaiah challenges the people to put their trust in God and to live public and private lives that reflect that trust. Recurring themes in Isaiah include (1) justice and righteousness and (2) assurance of divine blessing upon the faithful and divine punishment upon the unfaithful.

The focus of this study unit is Isaiah's "call" narrative. Isaiah differs from other prophetic books where the call narrative opens the book (for instance, see Jer. 1:4–10). Despite this difference, Isaiah's

---

2. Dates are noted as B.C.E. (before the Common Era): the older label, B.C. (before Christ) shows a bias toward the Christian view of Scripture, which the newer designation avoids.

call narrative stands in the tradition of other narratives (for instance, see Exod. 3:1–4:17). Here, Isaiah's story follows an accepted pattern: he has an encounter with God, he is part of a ritual or action that validates his call, and he is commissioned by God to some action. His call is tied to historical events—the death of King Uzziah signals a change for Judah. Judah's independence has been on shaky ground for a while but Uzziah's death and Tiglath-pileser III's rise to power in Assyria converge to place Judah in danger.

But it is at the very time of Uzziah's death, a decisive turning point for Judah, that Isaiah sees God—on a throne, being worshiped by heavenly hosts. Isaiah's description highlights the awesome nature of God—God is powerful and holy. The throne, high and lofty, may be the site of the Ark of the Covenant. In the vision, the mere hem of God's garment fills the temple. The seraphs or "fiery beings" (a transliteration of the Hebrew) who guard the throne must cover their eyes as well as their "feet" or genitals. Even the heavenly attendants cannot look upon or appear naked before God. Their words of praise shake the temple and the place is filled with smoke (it is not clear what the source of the smoke is—it could be incense or other burnt offerings). In the midst of such awesome wonder, Isaiah recognizes that he is not worthy and declares, "Woe is me! I am lost . . ." Not only is he unfit to be in God's presence, he is afraid for his life.

In response to his admission of unworthiness— "I am a person of unclean lips"—one of the seraphs takes a lump of hot coal from the altar and touches the lips of the prophet as a ritual of cleansing. In this action, symbolic action we hope since the seraph would not touch the live coal but rather lifted it with tongs, Isaiah is now free to be a spokesperson for God. Isaiah is alive after being in the presence of God. At this point, God has not addressed Isaiah directly; we might assume that God observes the action with disinterest. In fact, the only conversation so far in the story is when the seraph absolves Isaiah of his guilt and sin and cleanses him.

When God speaks, God addresses the seraphs and wonders who will do God's work. Without hesitation, Isaiah volunteers his services: "Don't worry about it. Send me. I'll go!" It is not clear if Isaiah understands what he is volunteering to do; there has not been an agenda set forth, no strategies to enact, no message to be taken. Either Isaiah is impulsively overcome by his spiritual experience or he is dazed and confused. Perhaps he doesn't care—the experience is enough to compel him to do God's work, whatever it is. At any rate, Isaiah pipes up and God gives him the commission.

God's commission startles us and probably Isaiah as well. Isaiah is to do all he can to keep the people from hearing God's word! What? Yes—Isaiah is to keep the people *from* listening (see Isa. 6:10).

What a strange job God gives Isaiah. This powerful, awesome God doesn't want the people to repent and be healed. This God wants the people to endure the divine punishment. God's commission catches Isaiah by surprise. In response, he manages only a question, "How long, O God?" And God makes it clear that Isaiah's charge won't end any time soon—not until the cities are destroyed and all the people gone; not until the land is wasted and lifeless; not until all the vegetation is burned. Why on earth would God want to do this to the land and the people? God does not explain. We are left only with the divine commission that the people and the land must stand under divine judgment.

Earlier in the book, God states the divine lawsuit against Israel, calling on the heavens and the earth to hear the divine indictment (see Isa. 1:2).

And God's opening charges are inflammatory, to say the least: Judah is a "sinful nation, laden with iniquity, with children who do evil and deal corruptly, have forsaken God, and are utterly estranged" (see Isa. 1:4). Judah and Jerusalem surely are on the defensive since God is not holding back anything. And what awaits them if they don't repent is total destruction, which has already been started by their disregard for God's vision of community. In other words, Judah will reap what it sows and is responsible for its destiny. The divine speech focuses on God's actions and God's desire:

> When you stretch out your hands,
>   I will hide my eyes from you;
> even though you make many prayers,
>   I will not listen;
>   your hands are full of blood.
> Wash yourselves; make yourselves clean;
>   remove the evil of your doings
>   from before my eyes;
> cease to do evil,
>   learn to do good;
> seek justice,
>   rescue the oppressed,
> defend the orphan,
>   plead for the widow.
>   (Isa. 1:15–17)

God's speech mirrors what we find in Amos 5 and Micah 6. God calls for justice, and this first chapter reflects connections to both the Torah and priestly traditions of early Israel. God is willing to negotiate with Judah, but the terms are clear. The people must be willing to change or face the playing out of their choice (see Isa. 1:18–20).

God offers judgment and the possibility of blessing; the "if-then" nature of this speech takes us back to the covenantal relationship of Israel with God—each with responsibilities and privileges. God utters the divine case and sets the stage for Judah's response. God appears as defendant, judge, and jury; it seems that the case has already been tried. And we may be reluctant to embrace the God who threatens destruction as the penalty for disobedience. However, we believe God to be the only true impartial, objective, and fair judge of human actions and motives. God judges based on expectations that have been clearly defined. The Torah is clear about religious and communal life; the people's experience of and with God should be enough to convince them that there is life and power in living God's ways and will.

In Isaiah 1 and other prophetic texts, the estrangement and destruction are not predictions of the future but rather the statement of current reality. The people's failure to live up to covenantal expectations has already estranged them from God and each other. Here and elsewhere, worship and community life are bound—to worship God sincerely and authentically translates into acts of love and justice. In Isaiah 5, we find a series of woes (but translated "Ah" in the NRSV; the NIV retains the essence of the Hebrew *hôy*, "Woe") that deal with social injustice concerns: property acquisition (5:8), alcohol abuse (5:11), lying (5:18), arrogance (5:20–21), bribery (5:23). The rich landowners and the powerful elite especially are held responsible for the breach between the people and God because they do not recognize and honor God's authority and power. They reject God's teaching and despise God's word (see 5:24). The point is that one cannot worship God without also caring for neighbor. With these judgments, God rests the divine case for the moment.

In Isaiah 6, however, God doesn't want to hear the nation's rebuttal. Surely, Isaiah must wonder what he's gotten himself into; and not only that, but what is God up to with this commission? What makes this text powerful is that Isaiah is allowed to raise questions about God's decision. Isaiah doesn't refuse to do God's bidding, but he does raise an eyebrow. Also, Isaiah offers intercession for the people. "How long?" is also asked in several psalms of complaint and petition (Psa. 13:2; 75:5; 89:46; 90:13). God's first reaction is not a hopeful one—"I might rethink my decision, but not until all is destroyed!" But even in God's indictment, God holds out the possibility of hope: "The holy seed is its stump" (Isa. 6:13b)—even when all is gone, there remains a seed. Who knows but that seed is the beginning of new life and hope for Judah?

We might think of God's purging of the land and the people in the same way that the coal is used to cleanse Isaiah. Fire purifies and cleanses—Isaiah confessed that he is a person of unclean lips living in the midst of people of unclean lips. Perhaps the refining, purifying fire is God's way of cleansing the people.

What conclusion can we draw from this puzzling text? Here the lectionary use of the text doesn't help us much because the lection ends with Isaiah's words "Here am I, send me." We don't get to hear and wrestle with Isaiah's commission. Instead of preaching repentance, Isaiah is compelled to preach against it. Isaiah is to make his message such that the people will continue doing what they are doing with no mind to the consequences or repercussions. And so we are left to ponder what good will come from such judgment and condemnation.

As we think about the power undergirding social justice ministries, this story serves as a wake-up call. It provides space for us to think about our real motivations for the work we do—are we really concerned about the common good or are we looking for personal gratification or recognition? Do some things have to die in order for new life to emerge? Must all be destroyed before any can be raised up?

We are cautioned to remember that judgment and condemnation are never the last word with God. To think that God is only about anger and destruction is to miss the biblical and prophetic message—judgment is followed by hope. Even if the hope is embodied in a tiny seed, it is hope nonetheless. The biblical message is that God alone is in charge of the universe and of us.

In this short passage of Isaiah, we are reminded that God is wondrously awesome and awe-inspiring—God's presence fills the earth and heaven; God's word calls us to do unusual things to further God's purpose and intentions; God cares about us enough to enter into history and make God's presence known to us. Isaiah is able to perform his commission because he knows deep down inside that God means good for the land and the people. The visible evidence is not happy news; but Isaiah, because of his experience of God, understands that God must be up to something life-giving, even when Isaiah cannot see it. And so it must be for those who engage in social justice work. Without the undergirding of deep spirituality, we cannot sustain this work over the long haul. Before too long, we are tempted to give up and give in. The problems are overwhelming and the forces working against us too strong. But our motivation must not be ours alone; we must work out of a deep sense of call and commissioning by God. Only God can provide the sustenance we need to stay on track. Only God can keep us focused and dedicated to the work at hand.

We live in a world that is in perpetual turmoil. In all our wisdom and with all our technology, we still fight wars (legal and illegal ones); we still depend heavily on our own devices to manage our affairs; we still have not solved pressing social issues like poverty, hunger, homelessness, underemployment, inadequate education and health care for all; we still give in to our self-centered interests to the detriment of others; we still fear those who are different from us. So even in the twenty-first century, we need voices to speak up in the face of wrongs and injustice. It seems like we are on a path to destruction; who knows whether God will intervene or leave us to live the consequences of our decisions and choices. Many people are resigned to these being the "last days" when justice seems far away and impossible to achieve. Maybe things will run their course and we will be undone . . . woe is us! But, when it is all said and done, God is still asking the poignant question: "Whom shall I send and who will go for us?" God still waits for an answer.

REFLECTION QUESTIONS

1. How does your picture of God resonate with or differ from the description in Isaiah 6?

2. How do you understand sin and guilt? In what ways does God cleanse you of your sins and guilt? In what ways does

God cleanse the church of its sin and guilt? In what ways does God cleanse the United States of its sin and guilt?

3. What is God calling you to *do*? What is God calling you to *be*? How do you know this?

4. Do you think Isaiah wishes he had not volunteered to do God's work? Why or why not?

5. How do you handle difficult situations? What alternative strategies might you consider?

2

Good News, Bad News

READ:

Isaiah 61:1–11

FOCUS TEXT:

*Do not remember the former things, or consider
the things of old. I am about to do a new thing; now it
springs forth, do you not perceive it? I will make a
way in the wilderness and rivers in the desert.*

(Isa. 43:18–19)

In ancient days, Israel was told by God to remember. Not only remember, but to tell their children, and their children's children, and
those children's children. Memory is a precious thing to the people
of Israel. And what memories they hold—of oppression and
bondage in Egypt; of a miraculous deliverance by a God whose
cryptic name leaves the people breathless; of a wilderness wander-
ing where the people bicker and murmur and long to return to the
security of the Egyptian Empire; of finally reaching the promised
land only to find people already there and unwilling to give up their

territory; of wars and rumors of war and God's charismatic leaders who save the day; of the early monarchy and David's strategic leadership; of the oppressive regime of Solomon, whose taxation laws send many people into debt, hocking their children as collateral; of a divided nation, one in the north and one in the south; of Assyrian armies marching against Samaria and taking Israel; of Babylonian armies marching against Jerusalem and taking Judah; of Persian marching armies and monarchs who allow the exiled Jews to return to Jerusalem. Some of these memories the people would rather forget. But as an African proverb so aptly states, "Those who do not know their history are doomed to repeat it." And so, Israel remembers. As they remember, they lament, mourn, and bewail their fate and destiny:

> By the rivers of Babylon—
>   there we sat down and there we wept
>   when we remembered Zion.
> On the willows there
>   we hung up our harps.
> For there our captors
>   asked us for songs,
> and our tormentors asked for mirth, saying,
>   "Sing us one of the songs of Zion!"
> How could we sing [YHWH]'s song
>   in a foreign land?
>   (Psa. 137:1–4)

In Isaiah 43, God encourages the people to move on and let go of the painful memories of the past. God is about to do a new thing—something that's never been done before. Of course, the last time the people heard that, they ended up in exile. What is God about to do now?

Isaiah 61 opens with a familiar passage. No doubt, this text from "Third Isaiah" (also Trito-Isaiah) sounds familiar. How many sermons based on this text have you heard? This text is used for ordination services and whenever the concern is for ministries of social justice. However, some may be surprised to find this text in the Hebrew Bible. This is the text that Jesus quotes in Luke 4:14–21 when he announces his call to ministry. We may wonder why Jesus quotes Isaiah. Jesus' words and action are not pulled out of thin air. His call is rooted and grounded in his faith tradition and his understanding of that tradition.

The history of Israel's relationship to God brings them to the moment that Isaiah critiques. The people have enjoyed a golden age of independence and power in spite of the monarchy that replaced God as the sole sovereign over Israel. The people rely on the monarchy to take care of them. Yet the people are always held to the covenantal agreement—they are to worship only God and to love their neighbor as themselves. Throughout their journey with God, God's people know God to be the Holy One who delivers, feeds, provides water, guides with pillars of fire and clouds. God sojourns with God's people and asks that they worship God and live as a community.

The division of the book of Isaiah into three sections is based on the differences in setting and content. Most scholars concede that the sixty-six books of Isaiah represent different voices and historical periods in the life of ancient Israel, even though we cannot identify the voices with any specificity. Chapters 40–66 were once believed to comprise one major section; today that premise is questioned. In general terms, in "Second Isaiah," we find the prophet dealing with the concerns of those in exile, while "Third Isaiah" is concerned with the post-exilic life of those who returned to Jerusalem under the leadership of Cyrus, the Persian monarch. After Assyria's and Babylon's rise to superpower status, Persia replaces them on the world landscape. Cyrus's understanding of empire differs from that of the Assyrian and Babylonian rulers. Cyrus allows any Judeans who so desire to return to their homeland, and a number of them take the offer.

The situation in Jerusalem is filled with tension between those who never left and those who return with their new ways of seeing the world and new understandings of Judean faith and religion. Of course, the lines marking the division between Second and Third Isaiah are not clear, so we can only speak in general, broad terms in our attempts to distinguish between the two.

So, although we notice a shift in tone in Isaiah 40, the tenor that is established in the first thirty-nine chapters of the book continues. Isaiah 40, which is set in the context of the heavenly council (as in Isa. 6), opens with words of comfort and implies that the judgments of Isaiah 6 have been accomplished and God is ready to move on:

> Comfort, O comfort my people,
>   says your God.
> Speak tenderly to Jerusalem,
>   and cry to her
> that she has served her term,
>   that her penalty is paid,
> that she has received from [YHWH]'s hand
>   double for all her sins.
>   (Isa. 40:1–2)

The shift is from the horrors of destruction and devastation (exile) to the expectation and hope of life to come always suggested in the first section of the book. The people who are kept blind and silent in Isaiah 6 are now to be consoled; the city set for destruction is now poised for restoration. A number of things have happened in the life of Judah—Jerusalem has been judged through the power of Assyria and Babylon; the people have been captured and dispersed throughout the empires—the worst that could happen has happened. Now, God is about to do a "new" thing because the "former" things have passed away (read Isa. 40:3–5).

God's new thing will shake things up and reorient the earth and people's understandings about the power and nature of God. Even in the midst of exile—desert and wilderness—the people must be prepared for the unexpected; a necessary and warranted judgment ultimately leads to restoration and hope. Those captured may return home and the entire world sees it. This speaks not so much to the benevolence of the Persian monarchy as it does to the will and sway of God who makes all things new and possible.

Through the prophet, God makes the divine expectation clear. The prophet states his call and commission—he is anointed and filled with the divine spirit. The prophet's mission is to bring good news, to bind up, to proclaim liberty and release, to proclaim the year of God's favor, to comfort, to provide for the mourners, to give garlands, the oil of gladness, and mantles of praise. Instead of making the people dumb and unaware, the prophet now comforts the afflicted, the oppressed, the imprisoned, the mourners—all who suffer now have comfort, solace, and hope. All who remember the "former things" now have something else to look forward to: total restoration and salvation for the faithful. Those who inflicted pain and destruction will repay Israel for its shame (see 61:5–7). The rest of the chapter deals with covenant issues of justice and integrity. The poetry is beautiful and the promises are guaranteed for generations to come. The nations bring gifts and render service to the once shamed Israel—what a marvelous restoration.

God's instructions about the nature and character of this community seem simple enough. There is to be a strong sense of the communal and the collective. This new community is to be characterized by three qualities:

- Justice (*mišpāṭ*): God's order for the whole of creation and in every area of life that is marked by fairness and impartiality.

- Loyalty (*ḥesed*): sometimes translated loving kindness or mercy; a covenant concept where God's love and care are everlasting and God is patient; the people are to be faithful to their covenant with God and others.

■ Compassion (*raḥamim*): caring for others out of a sense of gratitude for one's own blessings and a sense of being connected to others.

God makes provisions by holding the people responsible for *and* accountable to God. God challenges the Israelites to be good stewards and good neighbors (see Isa. 58:6–9a). But time and time again before the exile, the people failed to live up to their end of the deal. Under Saul, David, and Solomon, Israel became more like the nations surrounding it—property and goods were less communal and more concentrated in the hands of a few; people's labor was taken for granted, leaving open the possibilities of exploitation and abuse; the people were heavily taxed to bankroll royal lifestyles, to support the military, and to pay for infrastructure projects.

During the monarchy, things changed for everyone—landowners became rich and worked to maintain their status; the monarch consolidated power by establishing a bureaucracy; the common folk fell further and further behind financially, sometimes sending their children into indentured servitude to stave off bankruptcy. Until this point, poverty had been brought about through a setback or by chance (such as bad crops, bad weather). The poor could be helped out of poverty by the resources of the community. But the monarchy made poverty something else. The rich treated the poor as inferior and sought to protect their own resources instead of sharing. The poor became despised, ignored, and neglected. It was a Catch-22 or vicious cycle: as well as being poor, the poor were trapped, oppressed, exploited, *and* seen as inferior.

Charity is a virtue that is to be based on remembering Israel's days of bondage. It is the duty of the rich to help the poor, of the strong to protect the weak, of the monarch to care for all. Instead, the victims are blamed for their situation; the dignity and worth of the oppressed are discounted and stripped from them. In Jesus' day, the rich are seen as avaricious and greedy; the poor are seen as persons hardly able to maintain their honor and dignity. The rich control and have access to the necessities of life not available to the poor, or rather, withheld from the poor.

The moral problem is the essential wickedness of the rich who choose greed over God. They may be "nice" persons but their unwillingness to care for those in need is seen as poor stewardship and sinful. So, it is against this backdrop that Isaiah and Jesus declare their ministries. If Isaiah and Jesus had only themselves to rely upon, they would be in serious trouble. But they are under God's Spirit and anointed for their work.

God still needs persons willing to do the work of building God's realm—there remain in our midst and in places far away those who need to hear good news, brokenhearted folks who need a shoulder to lean on, captives and prisoners who long for freedom, sorrowful sisters and brothers who need garlands and oil and mantles. We don't have to look far to see the needs of others. And what is God calling us to do? What anointing do we need to hear the cries of those who long for justice and freedom? Perhaps they are:

- Migrant workers who travel according to the harvests and live sometimes dozens to a motel room without kitchens. They are often forbidden to bargain collectively for better pay and adequate and safe working conditions;

- Immigrants who seek better lives across language and cultural barriers;

- African Americans trapped by a system that withheld their forty acres and a mule and refuses to talk about reparations;

- Latino/as whose native languages are outlawed;

- Those isolated in rural areas without adequate family planning, health and education services and resources;

- Those who work in chicken plants where their hands are cut and fingers sliced and are denied health benefits;

- Sisters and brothers in developing countries who have no clean water, no adequate shelter, no access to medicine or education;

- Native American Indians imprisoned on reservations and whose hope rests on alcohol, tobacco, and casinos;

- The elderly whose children warehouse them and whose pensions are not enough to sustain them;

- Children around the world—sold, abandoned, forced into prostitution;

- Those caught up in the frenzy of materialism, consumerism, and supersizing, and craving more, more, more;

- Those who are forced off of public assistance and who have food stamp allowances reduced;

- Those whose factory jobs have been outsourced overseas and whose farms have been taken over by agribusinesses and multinationals;

- The working poor, the invisibles, who harvest our food, clean our offices, sew our clothes, and wash our cars, who seek not a handout but an opportunity, who see their lot as their own fault, who watch the rich get richer as they themselves pray to hit the lottery.

In Isaiah, we hear God's call and wait for God's anointing. Isaiah reminds the people that for God, it is always people first. And those of us who have resources at our disposal are not to hoard them or use them for our own self-interest. God calls us to use those resources to help those who are being crushed—to bring good news to the oppressed, to bind up the brokenhearted, to proclaim liberty for the prisoners, to give mourners garlands instead of ashes, oil of gladness instead of sorrow. God calls us into community, where we stand in solidarity with those who hunger and thirst for good news. As the church, we are heirs to Israel's promise from

God. We have much work to do in order to co-create God's beloved community characterized by justice, loving kindness and compassion. God wants to do a new thing—will we accept God's anointing and spirit?

REFLECTION QUESTIONS

1. In what ways are you anointed by God for special work? In what ways do you resist God's call, anointing, and Spirit?

2. Who are the oppressed, brokenhearted, prisoners and mourners in your local context? In what ways do you stand in solidarity with them to correct oppressive situations and conditions?

3. In what ways are you oppressed, brokenhearted, imprisoned and sorrowful? Who or what sustains and supports you in the midst of these death-dealing situations and conditions?

4. What does the "beloved community" look like in your context?

5. What ministries does your church and/or community offer to those in need? In what ways are you involved in these ministries?

3

Fire in the Bones

READ:

Jeremiah 1:1–19

FOCUS TEXT:

Now the word of [YHWH] came to me saying,
"Before I formed you in the womb I knew you, and
before you were born I consecrated you;
I appointed you a prophet to the nations."

(Jer. 1:4b–5)

FOCUS TEXT:

"Now I have put my words in your mouth.
See, today I appoint you over nations and over kingdoms,
to pluck up and to pull down, to destroy and to
overthrow, to build and to plant."

(Jer. 1:9b–10)

Poor Jeremiah! Or, in prophetic formula, "Woe is Jeremiah!" If ever there was a prophet who just didn't want to respond to God's call, it would be Jeremiah. He's almost as bad as Moses when it comes to finding excuses to say no (see Exod. 3:11, 13; 4:1, 10). Even after giving in to God's command, Jeremiah continues to whine and complain—and with good reason. Imagine speaking to the powers that be about plucking up, pulling down, destroying, and overthrowing—that's treason every day of the year. But that's Jeremiah's charge and he suffers greatly for accepting God's commission.

Of all the prophetic books, Jeremiah is the most difficult to grasp—there are just too many voices, sudden shifts from prose to poetry, confusing timelines, and theological perspectives to keep straight. The structure of the book may be a reflection or symbol of the chaotic times in which Jeremiah lived and prophesied. And of all the prophets, we see more of Jeremiah the person than the others. We feel that we know him because he is so open and candid about his feelings—indeed, he is popularly known as the "weeping prophet." He embodies the pain and suffering of devastation and exile; he also embodies hope in the midst of hopelessness—his own life (and that of his people) is about tearing down in order to build up again.

Jeremiah is identified as a descendant of the priest Abiathar who joined David's band of outlaws and was rewarded with an appointment in the royal court. His post as chief priest was rescinded when he supported Adonijah over Solomon in the struggle for the throne (see 1 Kings 2:26–27). Jeremiah's ministry is dated from 627 to 580 B.C.E. The book of Jeremiah is a collection of prophetic oracles against Judah and Jerusalem. His ministry begins with the religious reforms of Josiah, monarch of Judah. While figuring out a way to pay the workers who are repairing the Temple, Josiah is told of a find—the book of the law. Shaphan, the monarch's secretary, begins reading from the scroll; Josiah recognizes it and reacts quite dramatically (see 2 Kings 22:8–11). To be sure of the find, Josiah appoints a delegation of important leaders to verify his suspicions with confirmation of a trusted prophet.

The delegates pay a visit to the prophet, Huldah. In the text, she is carefully identified as a competent and trustworthy prophet (for her story see my *More Bad Girls of the Bible* [Cleveland: Pilgrim Press, 2009], 63–69). She confirms Josiah's suspicion; the scroll is, indeed, the book of Deuteronomy, and Judah is in serious trouble. And although his actions will not change the course of history for Judah, Josiah initiates a massive reform program. He assembles the entire people and reads the scroll, conducts a covenant renewal ritual, and recommits himself and the people to God (read 2 Kings 23:1–3). In addition, he commands a thorough cleansing of the Temple and the dismantling and destruction of all traces of Baal worship in Jerusalem, throughout out Judah, and even in parts of the northern territory, Israel. Those priests of the high places (alternative worship sites, often dedicated to Baal or Asherah) who refuse to come to Jerusalem are killed. As a final act of contrition and recommitment, Josiah reinstitutes the Passover festival and requires all to gather in Jerusalem for the festival.

Josiah's reforms, though, are not to be the rule of the land for long. He is soon killed by Neco, the pharaoh of Egypt, whom Josiah is trying to stop from forming a coalition with Assyria in an anti-Babylonian campaign. After Josiah's death, Judah steamrolls to its doom. Josiah's son, Jehoahaz, becomes the next Judean monarch; he is captured after only three months in office and deported to Egypt, where he dies (2 Kings 23:32–34). Pharaoh replaces Jehoahaz with another of Josiah's sons, Eliakim (and changes his name to Jehoiakim). The tides have clearly turned for Judah—instead of God's anointing a monarch, now the ruler in Egypt determines who the leader of Judah is. Jehoiakim holds office for eleven years and heavily taxes the people to pay his tribute to the monarch of Egypt.

But even this arrangement is not to last; Babylonian power grows and grows. The Babylonian monarch, Nebuchadnezzar, captures Egypt and effectively ends its dynasty. After an initial victory over Judah and over Egyptian territories, Babylonia loses control but quickly regains its military holdings. Nebuchadnezzar sends a coalition of military forces that include the Chaldeans, the Arameans, the

Moabites, and the Ammonites to take Judah. The massive siege can only be explained as the work of God (read 2 Kings 24:3–4). God is in control of Judah's destiny—having promised an eternal dynasty to David and eternal existence for Jerusalem, God has some questions to answer regarding Judah's current situation.

The people helplessly watch as Nebuchadnezzar ransacks Jerusalem—he raids the Temple and royal palace, taking silver, gold, and fine vessels. He ships out the monarch and his family, officials and dignitaries, priests and other important people. The only ones left in Jerusalem are the poorest people and Jeremiah is among their ranks. The city gates and wall are destroyed, announcing to the world that Judah is no longer an independent political entity. Jeremiah witnesses the destruction of the Temple and the dispersal of the people throughout the Babylonian Empire. Nebuchadnezzar, a brilliant military and political leader, appoints Mattaniah (and changes his name to Zedekiah) to govern Judah. Zedekiah is the last ruler of Judah. Jeremiah is on the scene to witness the destruction and devastation of Jerusalem and Judah.

The opening words of the book of Jeremiah identify him as a prophet of God and provide his call narrative. Jeremiah resides in Anathoth, north of Jerusalem and the home of the levitical priests (see Josh. 21:18). According to the text, Jeremiah is one in a long line of religious leaders and, as such, he knows the Mosaic traditions of Israel. His lineage, though, does not protect him when his kinsfolk turn on him (see Jer. 11:21–23). Jeremiah prophesies from about 627 to 587 B.C.E.—in that span, he sees and experiences a roller-coaster ride of ups and downs, including the life-giving reforms of Josiah to the death-dealing exile. The opening words give a clue that things will not end up well for Judah.

The word of God comes to Jeremiah and discloses God's purpose and mission for the prophet. It is clear that Jeremiah does not take up the role of prophet as a whim—he is called even before his birth. And he is called to preach to the nations—quite a task, to say the least. Not only that, when he attempts to protest, God mildly chastises him:

> But [YHWH] said to me,
> "Do not say, 'I am only a boy';
> for you shall go to all to whom I send you,
> and you shall speak whatever I command you,
> Do not be afraid of them,
> for I am with you to deliver you,
> says [YHWH]."
> (Jer. 1:7–8)

Jeremiah is not given a choice—he is chosen, commissioned and anointed. God knows him, inside and outside, and finds him worthy of the charge. He is to be about God's business. No one can honestly question Jeremiah's credentials or authority—his power comes from God. And his assigned area is not just to the people of God, it is wherever God declares. Usually prophets are commissioned to deal with internal concerns—social, political, economic, and religious dealings of the people of God. However, Jeremiah is to speak to communities outside of Judah. His words are spoken to Israel and Samaria, Judah and Jerusalem, as well as foreign nations. Jeremiah has an overloaded job description and we can't blame him for protesting. Jeremiah complains throughout the book that his calling is too much and is burdensome. His initial protest is because he is so young—he feels inadequate and too inexperienced to be of good use for God. But his protest is quickly squashed by God. It doesn't matter to God that Jeremiah is young—God will equip him for the work at hand. In fact, Jeremiah never has to worry because God is in control. All Jeremiah has to do is make himself available to God. It may seem a glamorous thing to be called by God. But when we see what Jeremiah's mission is, we do not envy him.

The message of Jeremiah is about how God moves in the human realm. God engages in destructive and constructive ways and brings balance to divine activity: to pluck up and pull down; to destroy and overthrow; to build and plant. There is judgment as well as renewal; there is destruction as well as redemption; there is an end as well as a new beginning. The book of Jeremiah is concerned about rewards and punishments, the just fruits of goodness and evil, and faithfulness and disobedience. Jeremiah attacks idol worship and emphasizes the need for repentance. He challenges the people to renew their commitment to God's covenant with their hearts.

What can we learn from Jeremiah's call narrative? Among the lessons is that God calls whom God chooses and equips the called for the work God has in store. God calls young and old, strong and weak—anyone can be called to do God's work. Another lesson is that our hesitancy is based on our insecurities rather than on God's capacity to make things happen. God knows us intimately and knows what we need to do the work God has for us. Another lesson is that God gives us work to complete; we need not be jealous or envious of others. God has enough work for everyone and God uses our unique gifts when they are needed. God has heard every excuse in the book and those called do not waver for lack of strength or power. In fact, when we are scared, God declares, "fear not! Just do it":

Have you not known? Have you not heard?
[YHWH] is the everlasting God,
    the Creator of the ends of the earth.
[The Holy One] does not faint or grow weary;
    [God's] understanding is unsearchable.
[God] gives power to the faint,
    and strengthens the powerless.
Even youths will faint and be weary,
    and the young will fall exhausted;
but those who wait for [YHWH] shall renew their strength,
    they shall mount up with wings like eagles,

> they shall run and not be weary,
>> they shall walk and not faint.
>> (Isa. 40:28–31)

Jeremiah's call sustains him through the trials and tribulations of his vocation. Every time he challenges God, he is met with reasons for his faithfulness to God's call. Jeremiah's very call places him in opposition to others in his community. He often feels isolated, alienated, threatened and lonely. In some instances, he is in real danger; other times, he dramatizes the burden of his call. But he has to do what God says, not because he is intimidated or coerced but rather because he understands his call too well. When he has no one else to turn to, Jeremiah turns to God and expresses the raw emotions of one who is scared, weary, frustrated, and sorrowful. Jeremiah is not shy about praying earnestly to God. He lifts up personal laments seeking God's help and each is followed by a divine response of retribution (see Jer. 15:10–21; 17:14–18; 18:18–23; and 20:7–18).

For instance, in Jeremiah 11:19–20, Jeremiah describes himself as a gentle lamb led to the slaughter, as a tree about to be destroyed. He does not know the plot is against him at first; but God makes him aware of the real threat against his life; Jeremiah's solution is clear:

> But you, O [YHWH] of hosts, who judge righteously,
>> who try the heart and the mind,
> let me see your retribution upon them,
>> for to you I have committed my cause.
>> (Jer. 11:20)

Jeremiah holds God accountable for his situation of danger and gives God an ultimatum—God's integrity is on the line here and God responds to Jeremiah's plea (see Jer. 11:21–23). God's solution is to blot out the plotters, who happen to be Jeremiah's kinfolk in Anathoth! The plot is not just against Jeremiah, it's against God, too. In

Jeremiah 12:1–4, Jeremiah carries on his argument and raises some poignant questions: why do the guilty prosper and the treacherous thrive? All Jeremiah is trying to do is God's work, but those who scheme and plot against him are not held accountable. The issue of theodicy is a theological challenge that we continue to confront today.

We often realize who our prophets are when they are dead—we shake our heads and bemoan that the good die young, while the wicked live to ripe old ages. We want justice and we want it now. God's response to Jeremiah leads us to believe that our prayers for retribution will be answered. We seek to understand why there is so much injustice in the world and why God doesn't do something decisive. We don't get the answers we seek; there is no denial that such questions are part of the human experience—we find the question in Job, the Psalms, and the Prophets. The Bible assumes that God is the question and the answer—we pray to God and trust that God is, indeed, in control. We trust that evil, wickedness, tragedy, and despair are not the final answer—God is.

We do not undermine our faith by asking the hard questions; nor do we water down our faith when we bemoan the absence of God in trying situations. While we may never know why the righteous suffer, we can know that God hears and cares. Perhaps that is enough. We know that Jeremiah stays the course despite all the threats he endures. When he tries to disengage from his prophetic vocation, he can only reaffirm his commitment:

> O [YHWH], you have enticed me,
>   and I was enticed;
> you have overpowered me,
>   and you have prevailed.
> I have become a laughingstock all day long;
>   everyone mocks me.
> For whenever I speak, I must cry out,
>   I must shout, "Violence and destruction!"

For the word of [YHWH] has become for me
    a reproach and derision all day long.
If I say, "I will not mention [God],
    or speak any more in [God's] name,"
then within me there is something like a burning fire
    shut up in my bones;
I am weary with holding it in,
    and I cannot.
    (Jer. 20:7–9)

May we, too, find our calling that is like fire shut up in our bones and our very being!

REFLECTION QUESTIONS

1. Describe your relationship with God; how do you communicate with God? How does God communicate with you? What is the quality of your relationship?

2. Describe the content of your prayers to God. Are they superficial or deep? Do you have seasons of earnest prayer? What determine these seasons?

3. Have you ever resisted a call from God? What are your reasons for the resistance? What was the outcome of your resistance?

4. Have you ever prayed for retribution or punishment for someone who has offended you? Explain.

5. Do you believe God punishes bad people? Will the wicked pay for their deeds? Why or why not?

4

Words Written on the Heart

READ:

Jeremiah 31:31–34

FOCUS TEXT:

But this is the covenant that I will make with the house of Israel after those days, says [YHWH]: I will put my law within them, and I will write it on their hearts; and I will be their God, and they shall be my people.

(Jer. 31:33)

The prophet Jeremiah goes through the pangs of preaching a word to people who really don't want to hear his message. He becomes so frustrated that he prays to God, asking why he has been chosen to do such an impossible job. His efforts are met with resistance and plots on his very life. In Jeremiah's eyes, the people are stubborn and stiff-necked—that is, they refuse to pay attention or heed Jeremiah's words. They prefer to do things their way and react hostilely towards Jeremiah. Jeremiah's work isolates and alienates him from the very people to whom he preaches. And every time Jeremiah seeks to be released from his work, he is further compelled to do God's work.

We have seen that Jeremiah's motivation is embedded in his bones—the fire of God's Spirit leaves him little choice. It is good that Jeremiah is able to express himself. He is open with his raw emotions and desires to do something else with his life. But once God gets a hold of us, we are held, for sure.

And just what does God want? The people try to appease God as people have tried to appease gods in the past—they perform rituals and ceremonies; they recite creeds and formulas; they make liturgical and proper pleas—but this God of Israel and Judah never seems satisfied. We learn that God is not impressed with perfunctory, empty gestures of appeasement. What God really wants is a people committed and passionate about their relationship to God.

Jeremiah tries and tries to tell them—their failure to love God with their whole lives is the problem; their failure to love their neighbor as themselves is the other part of the problem; their failure to establish and maintain right relationships with all of creation is still another part of the problem. God wants a people who understand and embrace the covenant that God extends as unmerited grace. But the people God chooses breach the covenant and are left to deal with the consequences of their choice. The people may not have the covenant burning in their bones like Jeremiah, but they should be totally committed.

It is difficult to stay committed to a God who seems to have fled the scene. The people have always known God to be present and powerful. But now, in the greatest challenge facing God's chosen people, God refuses to help. In fact, God not only allows the threat but also encourages it. And poor Jeremiah is the messenger:

> I spoke to King Zedekiah of Judah in the same way: Bring your necks under the yoke of the king of Babylon, and serve him and his people, and live. Why should you and your people die by the sword, by famine, and by pestilence, as

[YHWH] has spoken concerning any nation that will not serve the king of Babylon? Do not listen to the words of the prophets who are telling you not to serve the king of Babylon, for they are prophesying a lie to you. I have not sent them, says [YHWH], but they are prophesying falsely in my name, with the result that I will drive you out and you will perish, you and the prophets who are prophesying to you. (Jer. 27:12–15)

God tells Jeremiah to put on a yoke and strap it to his neck as a symbol for Judah's submission to the Babylonians (Jer. 27:2). Jeremiah's prophetic act highlights that submission is inevitable not only for Judah but for other nations, too. There is no escape from the Babylonians—they are powerful, strong, and smart.

The Babylonian Empire (the region is Babylonia and its capital city is Babylon) was one of the largest in ancient times; its border included the northern end of the Euphrates River with its prime location of major trade routes. Babylonia was a cosmopolitan center steeped in intellectual and judicial traditions. Babylonian monarchs dealt decisively with Egypt, Assyria, and other nations in the region. It remained a superpower until the rise of Persia.

As Babylonia makes its move on Judah, Jeremiah encourages the leaders to give in. He goes on to tell the people they should assimilate into the economic, agricultural, and culture aspects of the Babylonian Empire. The Babylonian threat is part of God's judgment and is to be accepted. However, acceptance is not forever. God will deliver God's people—but only after the judgment has played itself out. Jeremiah tells the people to make the best of a bad situation—take it and know that God ultimately will make things right for them. Jeremiah's word is for those in exile as well as those left in Jerusalem—all suffer the judgment and all will be restored. To those already deported, Jeremiah writes a letter and tells them to live as if they are still free:

> Thus says [YHWH] of hosts, the God of Israel, to all the exiles whom I have sent into exile from Jerusalem to Babylon: Build houses and live in them; plant gardens and eat what they produce. Take wives and have sons and daughters; take wives for your sons, and give your daughters in marriage, that they may bear sons and daughters; multiply there, and do not decrease. But seek the welfare of the city where I have sent you into exile, and pray to [YHWH] on its behalf, for in its welfare you will find your welfare. (Jer. 29:4–7)

They are to live their lives "as if" they are still in Jerusalem. The rhythms of life do not change even though their locale and situation have. They are to carry on business as usual, within the limits of the empire in which they find themselves. In this way, the people embody the hope that God has a word for them beyond exile and judgment. Jeremiah's words reflect his prophetic vocation—to tear down and build up. Now that the people have been torn down (are in exile), now they should live to build up—even in exile, they are to live in the hope of a future where family, freedom, and productivity are possible. In addition, they are to pray for the well-being of the region—their survival depends on the survival of the empire. The people have a better chance of making it if the empire is at peace and not suffering because of war, famine, drought, plague, or other times of challenge.

As we can imagine, Jeremiah's message is not met with cheers. In fact, for a people as proud as Judah, Jeremiah's message borders on treason—of course, the demise of the nation Judah precludes treason. But no one wants to hear Jeremiah's message to accept the fate of exile. Yet Jeremiah persists. God will revisit Judah and restore the nation, but only after the judgment and exile are fulfilled (read Jer. 29:10–14).

All they have to do is hold on—hold on until the change comes. The people are to live as people with hope for a future as yet not seen. In other words, they are to have faith that the God they have known in ages past is the same God who will bring them out of the gloom and shadows and back into the light. Jeremiah tells the people to live within the ambiguity of judgment and hope. It is not clear what the "seventy years" refers to; it may indicate a long period of time. It is likely that those in exile will not live to see the return to Jerusalem—but that is the point of faith. One is to live "as if" deliverance and restoration have happened. Christians are reminded in the book of Hebrews 11:1 that "faith is the assurance of things hoped for, the conviction of things not seen."

Those in exile are to live, not die prematurely by rebelling against the Babylonian Empire—this is a battle they cannot win. It is better to find a way to live within the system than to plot against it. Jeremiah gives the people a blueprint for survival; far from being treasonous, Jeremiah's message is one of hope, survival, and possibility. And their hope lies in once again being in God's city, Zion, Jerusalem. God is in control, still, of Judah's fate and destiny. Learning to live through the judgment and the exile will make the people stronger. And it is God's desire that through this experience of exile, the people will finally understand what it means to be God's people.

Our focus text in Jeremiah 31 is part of what is commonly known as "The Book of Consolation." This section of Jeremiah focuses on comfort and hope—after the harsh words and activity of judgment, God now offers a pastoral possibility: Judgment is not the final word. God's "new thing" is renewal and restoration. The experiences of exile are placed alongside the experiences of God—from ancient days to the present day. And the people will know God. God makes a new covenant with the people—one that is written on the heart so that they will not forget or break it. In the future, the people will obey the covenant because it is in their bodies—head, heart, and hands. They will not have to think about what to do, they will know and act accordingly. They will worship

YHWH with their whole hearts—their worship will be authentic and joyful; their rituals and ceremonies will be times of commemoration and not empty gestures. They will live in community that is characterized by love and a commitment to what is best for the community. They will care for the most vulnerable in the community and make sure that all have what they need to live good lives. They will follow the instructions of the Torah as a matter of fact and not subvert them for selfish reasons and concerns. All will have a place of dignity and worth in the community and none will suffer at the hands of others.

What does God want? A people fully committed to God and fully committed to each other. And not just a small group, but the entire cosmos—living in peace and harmony, exercising stewardship that does not exploit or abuse, loving and praising God as creator, redeemer, and sustainer of all life.

Jeremiah's vocation is a hard one. Not many of us are called to make the sacrifices he makes or to live a life of anguish and despair as he does. Most of us will live fairly comfortable lives. The demands of family and work and church will seem fairly reasonable and manageable. When we feel overwhelmed and pressured, we often have opportunities to take a time out to regroup. Many of us have solid support systems that help us get through difficult times. Jeremiah reminds us that we are not to take our ease for granted—for at any moment, life can take a turn that knocks us down. At any time, we may find ourselves in valleys of shadows and gloom; we may find ourselves in the depths of despair and hopelessness. At any time, we may be victims of powers and principalities over which we have no control. When life throws us a curveball, we are to remember that God still rules. That negative experiences and calamities are not the final word—God is.

The prophet Jeremiah tells us what God wants and expects: for us to know God and live "as if" God's covenant is written on our hearts.

REFLECTION QUESTIONS

1. Describe a time when you had to make a difficult decision. To whom did you turn for advice? Was the advice given helpful to you? What was the outcome of your decision? Explain.

2. Where do you find support? In what ways do you support others?

3. How did you interpret the events of September 11, 2001, when the twin towers of the World Trade Center were destroyed? Where was God in those events?

4. What message do you think God has for the United States given our foreign policies and practices? What message does God have for nations where there is strong U.S. military and economic presence and abuse of power?

5. What in your life needs renewal and restoration? What in your church and our nation stand in need of renewal and restoration?

5

Visions and Dry Bones

———

READ:

Ezekiel 37:1–14

FOCUS TEXT:

[YHWH] said to me, "Mortal, can these bones live?"
I answered, "O [YHWH], you know."

(Ezek. 37:3)

Despite its harsh message, the book of Ezekiel is a motion picture director's dream. Not only does the book lend itself to all kinds of psychological analyses, it also is perfect for computer-generated graphics and animation. Ezekiel is filled with vivid descriptions and impossible feats of power complete with sound effects. Ezekiel is victim to hallucinations and weird behaviors. With the opening lines (see Ezek. 1:1–3), we know we are in for quite a ride. Ezekiel sees visions, hears voices, and acts out his prophecies to the point where we wonder if he suffers some kind of mental illness. However, he is far from being delusional—he lives the very word of God and prophesies with power and clarity.

Ezekiel is a priest who is taken into captivity by the Babylonians in the first wave of deportations in 597 B.C.E. His profession as priest is disrupted and he is forced to travel with his fellow exiles to a foreign land away from the comforts of home. We can only imagine the angst he must feel as he now lives among people who do not believe in the same God, don't worship in the same ways as the Judeans, and don't care about their captives. And if this were not bad enough, Ezekiel preaches and ministers to people who are devastated at the turn of events that force them into captivity.

It is likely the exiles have tons of questions for the priest-prophet: how did this happen? Where is God? We thought God would never forsake or abandon us. What are we to do now? When can we go home? Is God unable to beat the Babylonians and their gods? Why have we followed a God who doesn't follow through with divine promises? Day after day, week after week, month after month, the questions come and Ezekiel has to figure out what to say.

Fortunately for him, God has all the words he will need. But God's words are difficult to hear and the people resist. And who can blame them? These are folks who believed *some* things would never change:

- That as God's chosen people, they would always enjoy God's covenantal blessings—God would always protect and care for them;

- That the land God promised their ancestors would never be taken away—God would always make sure they kept the land;

- That God's promise to David of an eternal dynasty would always stand—Judah could depend on Davidic leadership, no matter what;

- That the Temple Solomon built, which housed the very presence of God, would never be destroyed; God would not allow the divine homestead to be desecrated or destroyed.

These are the promises on which the people of Judah stand. They cannot even fathom a situation where any of these understandings would be compromised. And so it is with great dread and despair that they find themselves sojourning to a strange land, among strange people. Their worst fears have come to pass—God has, indeed, forsaken them, given them up to hostile powers. They watch helplessly as the walls of Jerusalem are torn down and the Temple raided and burned.

It is difficult for us to comprehend the depth of emotions the citizens of Judah are experiencing. For U.S. citizens, perhaps the closes analogy is the destruction of the twin towers of the World Trade Center on September 11, 2001. We watched in disbelief as the images of the planes barreling into the concrete and steel buildings were played over and over. We were horrified as we watched the towers teeter-totter and crash. We were stunned by the pictures of smoke and ash and debris filling the streets of New York City. We wept as we saw people running in terror and bodies strewn over the walkways and streets of the city. For days, we mourned the loss of innocent life and questioned where God was in all of the mayhem. We frantically tried to reach family and friends on the East Coast and lived through the frustration of not being able to connect. Those stranded in airports around the world wondered if there were more attacks on the way. As a nation, we were crippled for weeks trying to make sense of it all and trying to get back to a sense of normalcy. Many of us knew that we would never have normalcy again—in those early hours of September 11, things changed and would never be the same. Many words were spoken on that day and days following this catastrophe. A resounding question lingered in the air, "Why do they hate us so much?" Most asked not knowing the "they" of the question. When unexpected tragedy happens, we want to blame someone or something. Still we have no answers.

Another analogy may be found in the aftermath of Hurricane Katrina, which hit the southern coast of the United States in August 2005. The hurricane caused some $80 billion in damages and left nearly two thousand dead. Especially hard hit, and graphically so, was New Orleans when the levees gave way. Despite the efforts of city and state officials to evacuate the citizens, thousands were left with no recourse or resources to survive. The breached levees left us wondering how such a thing could happen in the twenty-first century in one of the most beloved tourist cities in the nation. We watched helplessly as the water took over the land and people waited on rooftops for helicopter rescues. We watched horrified at dead bodies and dead animals floating on the waters. We just couldn't believe our eyes at the conditions inside the Super Dome—the home to Super Bowls past. While the devastation swept across racial and class lines, many of us were appalled at the number of black people displaced and forgotten in New Orleans. Those who lost homes were labeled "refugees" in their own nation; they waited in vain for help and many perished for lack of shelter, food, and clean water. Some were able to get food supplies—the whites were survivors, the blacks were looters and thieves—underscoring the ongoing and growing gap among the races and their access to services. And a question continues—where was God in the midst of the devastation?

It seems a bit easier to deal with natural disasters—we can blame Mother Nature. We have more difficulty rationalizing human neglect, violence, and destruction, so we seek scapegoats. On September 11, 2001, the scapegoats were "terrorists" who hate the United States for no good reason, and in New Orleans, though unspoken, the scapegoats were poor blacks who were blamed for not evacuating despite the fact that many had not been informed about the evacuation, had no modes of transportation, were ill, or otherwise had no way of leaving the city. Of course, there is great irony in attempting to identify scapegoats—we can never be sure why things happen as they do. And that is the challenge for faith communities—making sense of that which actually makes no sense.

And this is the task of Ezekiel—as one in exile, how does he help others make sense of the impossible? Ezekiel, like other prophets, is unrelenting in his accusations. He holds the very people of God responsible for their own demise. He hides behind the commission of God, but his mission is a difficult one (read Ezek. 2:3–5). Ezekiel is both priest and prophet—he is to provide pastoral care and challenge the people!

On the one hand, he is to comfort the exiles and assure them of God's care and love. And at the same time, he is to condemn them for the actions that placed them in jeopardy in the first place. For Ezekiel, the sins of the people go back to their infidelity to God and God's covenant. Ezekiel's message is both religious and political. The people are to be holy as God is holy; adherence to the teachings of the Torah is the way to show their holiness. Ezekiel equates covenantal faithfulness with holiness. The people honor God and do not bring shame upon themselves or God. God is supreme and there is none like God. If the people really know this, they will behave in ways that give life to the Torah instructions—they worship only God and they love their neighbors as they love themselves. But time and time again, the people have failed. And this time, God has said, "Enough!"

Ezekiel tells the people that they have gone too far; God has no choice but to let them live out the consequences of their choices and decisions. The sins of the people are great and heinous—there can be no deliverance until a cleansing happens (see Ezek. 22:6–12). The catalog of wrongdoing is familiar: elders are disrespected; sojourners are exploited; orphans and widows are neglected; the Sabbath is violated; God's holy things are profaned; neighbors' wives are coveted; sexual assaults are rampant; leaders are bribed; innocent blood is shed—it's too much and God has had enough.

The prophet's indictment is devastating news—an already demoralized people are also humiliated. The victims are blamed for
their own victimization. But Ezekiel tells them that they brought it
upon themselves. God has shown them the way and they have continued to defy God and God's ways. The people can only lament,
weep, and wail:

> Then [God] said to me, "Mortal, these bones are the whole
> house of Israel. They say, 'Our bones are dried up, and our
> hope is lost; we are cut off completely.'" (Ezek. 37:11)

As we have seen and will see with other prophets, the word of
judgment is not the final word. It is as if God needs to get something off the divine chest—so God rants and raves, spews out
bitter punishment, and pretends that God is not moved by the
recalcitrance of God's people. God tries to be detached and mete
out judgment as a matter of fact. We suspect that in this case, the
punishment hurts God as much as it hurts God's people. After the
emotional tirade, God extends the possibility of redemption, compassionate care, and hope for the future.

Such is what we find in Ezekiel 37. Almost every preacher has
a "dry bones" sermon. The text practically preaches itself—the ca-
dence and images are stirring and vivid. We don't have to do much
to get the point. To a people who are in the depths of utter despair,
there is a word of hope and life.

In a vision, Ezekiel is taken by God to a valley filled with dried
and bleached bones. God leads Ezekiel so he cannot miss the sight
and stench of neglected human remains. The unburied bones sym-
bolize abandonment and neglect—not one bone holds any muscle
or skin. These bones are dead—really dead! And God asks Ezekiel
a profound question—can these bones live? Of course, any person
in their right mind knows the answer is a resounding "No!" There is
no way on earth these bones can live. But the cautious Ezekiel manages only, "Gee, God, only you know."

God tells Ezekiel to prophesy to the dead—really dead—bones. Ezekiel is used to strange requests from God, so he is not shocked at this latest request. And so he preaches to the bones—they find their mates and reattach themselves; the bones are held together by sinew and cartilage and muscles; the skeletons are covered with flesh and skin—the color comes back to ashen cheeks; lifeless limbs resume activity; eyes blink and noses twitch; hair blows in the wind—but still the bodies are like zombies.

Ezekiel is told to prophesy again summoning the four winds to breathe upon the lifeless bodies to make them whole and vibrant. And so it is that God's breath, *rûaḥ*, animates the zombies and they live. Ezekiel 37:9–10 takes us back to Genesis 2:7 where God animates the creature made from the dust. The dead bones live and stand.

Not only that, but God promises to reconstitute the people and will do so in their homeland (see Ezek. 37:12). For Ezekiel, God's action is not because the people deserve to be resurrected but rather because God's integrity is on the line. God declares that there are no other gods to be worshiped. God promises covenantal blessings upon the chosen people—yet, here they are in exile, as if they have no God powerful enough to protect them. But God is not done with the house of Israel and Judah—God intends to restore them (see Ezek. 37:12b–14).

God promises new life through a new exodus, this time out of captivity and exile back into the land promised to their ancestors. The judgment will be over and all can start fresh. Ezekiel hopes that the lessons of captivity and exile will create new hearts within the people and that they will be ready to really be God's people. Ezekiel envisions a reconstituted people, renewed inside and out, ready to rededicate themselves to God and God's ways.

Despite the trauma of watching his nation destroyed, the beloved Temple ransacked and torched, and the march into exile, Ezekiel never loses faith in God. He holds on to his faith and believes that God will heal the people and the land. Ezekiel does not doubt that God is able and willing to do marvelous things. Even in a valley of dead bones, Ezekiel does not question God's capacity to bring them back to life.

And so it is with us today. We don't have to look far to see dry bones in our midst. We have but to see and not just look; to hear and not just listen. If we pay attention to national and local policies and practices, we may find valleys of dry bones in our very back-yards. Our failing infrastructures, seemingly unlimited funds for war and defense, unaccountable bailouts for big businesses, inatten-tion to manufacturing innovations and research, the crumbling of our schools and lack of funds for adequate education for all of our children, the high cost of inferior health care, the loss of jobs to mar-kets that exploit workers—we don't have to look far to see valleys of dry bones. The devastating military presence and corporate ex-ploitation in nations whose names we cannot pronounce, the mur-der of civilians perpetrated by the U.S. government, the uncritical support of the Israelis and nonchalance for the plight of the Palestinians, the neglect of those barely surviving famine, drought, and HIV/AIDS in Africa—we don't have to look far to see valleys of dry bones. We don't need dramatic events like that of September 11, 2001, or hurricanes to get our attention. There are such valleys in the United States and around the globe.

And God continues to ask the question: can these bones live?

REFLECTION QUESTIONS

1. Why do you think God calls the priest Ezekiel to take on the tasks of prophet? What skill set does Ezekiel bring to his fel-low exiles?

2. What has been your experience of exile? Where did you turn for comfort and support?

3. How do you understand holiness? In what ways can the church embody holiness? What does holiness look like in everyday life?

4. What valleys of dry bones can you identify in your local context? How are you responding to the question, "Can these bones live?"

5. In what ways is God breathing new life into your life, your faith community, and the world? Explain your answers.

6

Locusts and Judgment

READ:

Joel 2:15–32

FOCUS TEXT:

Then afterward I will pour out my spirit on all flesh;
your sons and your daughters shall prophesy, your old men
shall dream dreams, and your young men shall see visions.
Even on the male and female slaves, in those days,
I will pour out my spirit.

(Joel 2:28–29)

God is going to pour the divine Spirit on everyone—sons, daughters, young, old, free, and slave! What a promising prospect and an opportunity. But what does it mean to be showered, splashed, smattered, drenched in God's Spirit? Are we ready for this outpouring? What can we expect? Should we not opt for something more subdued, more dignified, more subtle? Will we rant and rave like mad persons? Perhaps we will be empowered to do the work God wants us to do—to bring love and justice into a world that is clamoring for balance and harmony. Does Joel have a word for our time?

We don't know much about the prophet Joel. He is the son of
Pethuel, a name that only appears in the book of Joel. There is no
other biographical information in the opening verses of the book.
His name means "[YHWH] is God" and his words are given to him
by God. The book of Joel was probably composed while Judah was
a province of the Persian Empire. Scholars believe that the conditions alluded to in the book suggest that the Temple of Solomon has
been reconstructed (called the Second Temple) because the walls of
Jerusalem have been restored and the priests are active and make
daily sacrifices. There seems to be no outside threat to the realm.
However, there is no agreement about the precise date of the book.

Joel uses older Israelite traditions as the foundation for his message; he reworks the messages of earlier prophets to illuminate the
issues of his day. He suggests that older prophecies have yet to be
fulfilled and that God continues to work through prophets to get a
message to Judah. Further, Joel suggests that God's work reaches
into the future; therefore, Joel has a word for us today.

Through a series of poetic oracles, Joel talks about the "Day of
[YHWH]" a time of judgment as well as restoration. His central
image is that of a locust plague after which follows a drought. He
challenges the elders of Judah to share the story with future generations (see Joel 1:2–3). In the opening verses, Joel makes clear that
the locust plague devastated the land and placed Judah in a life or
death situation. In 1:4, the prophet uses adjectives to convey the
overwhelming results of the locust attack: cutting locusts, swarming
locusts, hopping locusts, and destroying locusts. Part of his task is
to help the people make sense of this threat to their survival—what
is God trying to tell Judah through the work of the locusts?

Joel calls the people to lament—they have reason to weep and
wail because their very survival is at stake. He uses luxurious language to convey how desperate the situation is for Judah. He com-
pares the locust plague to a powerful army that spares no one and
nothing in the land—all are utterly destroyed. And if locusts were

not enough, the people now suffer a drought that dries up the land and causes vegetation to wither before it can be harvested.

Joel calls the priests to lament and to proclaim a public fast. Joel is like the cartoon figures we see in magazines—bearded, gray, in sandals, carrying a sign that says, "Repent! The end is near!" Indeed, for Joel, the double whammy of the locusts and the drought can only be explained as the coming end of time. Joel uses the phrase "Day of [YHWH]" as a warning that the devastation is a sign that the people are disconnected from God. As we have seen in other periods of Israel's life, when the people disregard God and do their own thing, only tragedy is left.

Joel tells the priests that they, too, must shoulder some responsibility for the spiritual lapse in Judah; they, too, must lament, pray, and fast—none are exempt from the devastation and all must pull together to make things right with God. Joel tells the priests to summon and gather all the people to weep, wail, pray, and repent of their sins in the holiest place possible, the Temple.

Joel calls the leaders and people to return to the familiar—public and communal fasts were called whenever Israel was faced with a national disaster, including war, famine, and captivity. Such a fast requires the people to abstain from food, water, work—anything that distracts them from giving their full attention to God. Joel's vivid images leave us breathless—not only do the people suffer, but also plants and animals—"seeds shrivel . . . storehouses are desolate . . . granaries are ruined . . . animals groan . . . herds of cattle wander about . . . flocks of sheep are dazed . . . wild animals cry to [God]" (see Joel 1:17–20). The prophet challenges the priests to do as the wild animals do, cry out to God. In ancient times, people believed that God sent natural disasters to bring the people back to the divine. In this instance, the priests and people have forgotten what the wild animals have not—that prayers are to be lifted up to the only One who can fix things, God. Humans cannot rely on their own devices because such reliance only leads to death. God is the one who answers prayers, and so prayers for deliverance and restoration must be addressed to God.

Much of the dread people feel when they read the prophets is found in the opening verses of Joel 2—the "Day of [YHWH]" is described in striking and terrifying language; the day comes like marauding troops bringing with them deep shadows and gloom, devouring fire, desolate wilderness, war-horses, rumbling chariots, unrelenting fear, and entering through the windows of homes like thieves. The earth shakes and the heavens tremble, the sun and moon are obscured and the stars stop shining: "Truly the day of [YHWH] is great; terrible indeed—who can endure it?" (Joel 2:11c). The final judgment is nothing to laugh at—the enemy comes like the locusts in dreadful waves and Hollywood-type drama: the steady march into the city despite the wall of defense, scaling and climbing into windows, the crackling of fire and heat of flames. What is more, God shows up in the midst of the devastation; throughout the Hebrew Bible, God's presence causes disruptions both on earth and in the heavens. When God fights the enemy, the universe is affected. Joel uses familiar images to describe the last days. We do not know what the day of God's judgment will be like; we can only draw on the images of the prophets, who use those from earlier Israelite traditions. We are haunted by Joel's poignant question: "Who can endure it?" And that is the question. If we only have ourselves to depend and rely on, we surely cannot endure even a portion of the coming destruction. We wait with bated breath to see if Joel provides the key for survival.

The people of Judah just can't catch a break—first the locust plague, then the drought, and now the coming judgment of God. In the midst of despair, terror, and hopelessness, God is ready to extend mercy. Through Joel, God calls the people to return, re-turn or turn back, to true and faith-filled worship. God's invitation is filled with hope and love (see Joel 2:12–14).

During a lament, the people tear their clothes as a way of expressing grief, fear, or horror at some distressing event. The heart is the place of one's will—the people are asked to turn away from infidelity and apostasy and turn to God as an intentional act. This invitation mirrors that in Deuteronomy (6:6) and in other prophetic works (Jer. 4:4, Ezek. 18:31). God extends mercy and forgiveness in patient waiting. God's "steadfast love" (*ḥesed* in the Hebrew) is God's eternal honoring of the covenantal relationship with the people. The people have a chance to turn things around by turning *themselves* around. The if-then proposition stands as a possibility—if the people repent, then God will hear and respond. The prophet does not declare what God will do—Joel holds the hope that *maybe* God will show mercy. Given what the people know about the nature of God, that possibility is real and not an empty hope.

In Joel 2:15, the prophet again calls for the trumpet; only this time, the priests do not call the people to war but rather to a religious assembly—to prepare for worship. And this is not an optional activity; everyone is expected to show up—infants and the elderly, brides and grooms—all must be in attendance as the priests weep and pray to God on behalf of the assembly. The priests are to ask God to remember the covenantal relationship and save face among the other nations. We know, though, that God doesn't care much about saving face. God would rather be in relationship than look good—a lesson for our own relationships.

In this instance as in the past, the people are assured that if they turn back to God, God will be gracious and accept their repentance and rescue them. In every case, the hope is for God's mercy and grace with no guarantee of automatic benevolence. However, the people live in the hope that the God who has forgiven in the past will once again extend love and forgiveness. This assurance of hope is expressed in Joel 2:18–19, where curses are turned to blessings. If the people really and sincerely repent and turn back to God, the "Day of [YHWH]" becomes a day of deliverance and salvation. It is not clear who comprises the "northern army" in verse 20; some suggest it is the locusts, but locusts usually traveled from the south. Finally, we should read this to mean an agent of God's anger and judgment—God is willing to change God's mind from judgment to mercy.

In Joel 2:21–27, we see further reversals from judgment to salvation—the devastated land, the animals, the wilderness, the fruit trees, the empty storehouse, and the weeping and fearful people have been saved.

Today, we seek answers for natural disasters and attribute many things to global warming. We are noticing more floods and droughts, more viral and bacterial pandemics, more volcanoes and earthquakes—we are not sure if these are "normal" occurrences that are cyclical or if there is a real change in the way the earth is evolving. Some feel that global warming is simply the natural maturing of the earth—there are seasons for growth and death. We refuse to consider that we, too, are part of the circle of life. In the spring of 2009, the History Channel broadcast a series entitled *Life After People* in an attempt to imagine what the earth will be like when we are no longer here. Our monuments designed to immortalize our presence will crumble and disappear when we are no longer here to maintain them. Computer-generated images projected what our major cities and rural areas will look like after one year, ten years, one hundred, one thousand, fifty thousand years with no human life. The images are fascinating and help us to remember that we are part of creation—we are not the only part. At the very least, the television series helps us to understand the psalmist:

> When I look at your heavens, the work of your fingers,
>   the moon and the stars that you have established;
> what are human beings that you are mindful of them,
>   mortals that you care for them?
> (Psa. 8:3–4)

When we run out of scientific rationalizations, we turn to the heavens for answers. During times of tragedy, hurricanes, tornadoes, or wildfires, we can trace some human involvement; sometimes, these acts of nature are the result of insufficient attention to infrastructures or human error in construction or maintenance. Other times, there are no logical explanations and we ask why God allows these things to happen. Why does God allow the loss of human life? These questions seem to have no answers. We are left to ponder the wonders and ways of God. And we trust that God continues to care about and for us—so whatever happens, everything is in God's hands.

REFLECTION QUESTIONS

1. Joel uses the images of locusts and drought to describe the end of time. How do you imagine the last days? What images frame your understanding?

2. How does your faith community understand the presence and working of God's Spirit? How does your understanding resonate or go against that in Joel? Explain.

3. How does God move in your life? What does God's Spirit prompt you to do?

4. What is God up to in the world today as we discover the corruption of government, corporations, and religious leaders? What lessons do you think God wants us to pay attention to in these discoveries?

5. What legacy do you wish to leave for your family? Your church or faith community? For the wider society?

7

Waters and Streams

―――

READ:

Amos 5:21–24

FOCUS TEXT:

But let justice roll down like waters,
and righteousness like an everflowing stream.

(Amos 5:24)

How can anyone "like" the book of Amos? Taken on the surface, it is one of the most depressing books in the Bible. Amos moves from one disaster to the next without pausing—we are breathless and demoralized at the end of his rantings. His prophecies are strident indictments against the rich and powerful. His message is uncompromising—God's judgment will be the result of the people's acts of social injustice and religious arrogance.

Scholars generally agree that Amos is the earliest of the classic prophets. Amos prophesies during the reigns of two monarchs: Uzziah of Judah and Jeroboam II of Israel. Although a native of Judah (he hails from the small village of Tekoa, in the hills south of Bethlehem), Amos preaches to the northern nation Israel and its major cities of Samaria and Bethel. Amos preaches during a time of economic prosperity and military security; there are no major military threats and a small number of Israelites are doing quite well financially. But Israel's reliance on its military prowess, its shaky economic practices, and its superficial piety can only lead to its downfall. Imagine having to preach this when the good times are rolling.

As Amos observes the policies and practices of Israel, we notice some emerging ideas about how to understand poverty and wealth from a theological perspective:

- Prosperity is seen as God's blessing; a reward for obeying God's commands. Poverty and disaster are signs of God's negative response to infidelity. Prosperity now carries moral and religious meaning.

- The sense of justice moves the prophets to denounce all wealth gained at the expense of the poor. The prophets' protest is grounded in the belief that God rewards fidelity and punishes injustice. Because of the monarchy, wealth leads to power by which the poor are robbed of their rights.

- Since God will destroy the nation or allow it to be destroyed because of injustice to the poor (in addition to national idolatry and apostasy)—the expectation of the future world includes a vision of equity and prosperity for all and that the ideal ruler is the *gō'ēl* (redeemer) and champion of the poor.

- The just judge (*gō'ēl*) determines who is right and fixes the inequity of the case; God, who is committed to justice and righteousness, is especially concerned to fix the plight of the oppressed poor. Poor persons count on God to fix their situation—hence, they live in hope!

Thus, we can summarize the essence of justice by quoting from the prophet Zechariah (7:9b–10): "Render true judgments, show kindness and mercy to one another; do not oppress the widow, the orphan, the alien, or the poor; and do not devise evil in your hearts against one another."

For Amos, justice means doing the right things for the right reasons. Righteousness is living in ways that honor members of the community. Observing the covenant means that persons live according to the teachings of the Torah; anything else is a breach of contract and will bring judgment. Amos' challenge is preaching a message of justice during a period of ease and comfort; he has the task of shaking up the people enough for them to hear the message he brings from God.

Amos preaches judgment against "the nations" even though they do not come under the umbrella of the Torah. For God, and Amos, there are some basic human rights that are not to be violated by any nation. Failure to observe the rights of all leads to punishment. Amos declares in his indictments that God is the Creator of all nations and holds power over them. The list of cities and nations and their crimes are most interesting because both Israel and Judah are included in the list:

- Damascus, the capital of Syria (or the biblical Aram), is guilty of waging war against Gilead and will be devastated and its people sent into exile (Amos 1:3–5);

- Gaza, a city of Philistia, is guilty of enslaving communities and turning them over to Edom; Philistia's major cities of Ashdod, Ashkelon, and Ekron will perish (1:6–8);

- Tyre is guilty of turning over communities to Edom, against kinship connections, and will be burned (1:9–10);

- Edom is guilty of turning on its kinsfolk, and the city Teman will be burned and Bozrah captured (1:11–12);

- Ammon is guilty of human rights violations, and the city of Rabbah will be burned and monarch and other leaders sent into exile (1:13–15);

- Moab is guilty of war crimes against the monarch of Edom; the city of Kerioth will be destroyed and the nation will undergo a chaotic end that kills its monarch and other leaders (2:1–3);

- Judah is guilty of rejecting God's law and of idolatry; the city Jerusalem and the nation will be burned (2:4–5);

- Israel is guilty of exploiting the poor, sexual violations, and desecrating God's house; Israel will experience judgment and disaster (2:6–16).

In our Bible study text, Amos spells out in graphic detail the corrupt practices of grain tycoons, in league with the temple bankers, who tamper with the very life of the economy—the weights and measures and the valuation of the money. Through unjust economic practices, the poor are being exterminated:

> because they sell the righteous for silver,
>   and the needy for a pair of sandals—
> they who trample the head of the poor into the dust of the earth,
>   and push the afflicted out of the way;
> father and son go in to the same girl,
>   so that my holy name is profaned;
> they lay themselves down beside every altar
>   on garments taken in pledge;
> and in the house of their God they drink
>   wine bought with fines they imposed.
> (Amos 2:6b–8)

Ouch! While the other nations are bad, Israel is worse. The standard of justice is higher for God's people and they are acting like nations who have no God. The language is harsh and highlights the depths to which the nation is sinking. There is no accountability and no one calling for justice. God's judgment is going to be decisive. The people have ignored the warnings along the way—famine, drought, blight and mildew, locusts, pestilence, death of cattle and horses—none of these were seen as signs to repent. Therefore, God will bring judgment on the nation (see Amos 4:6–13).

The traditional days of religious observance and rest are merely tolerated by the merchants who resent these interruptions to their profit-making. Amos decries the rich getting richer and the poor getting poorer. He challenges the people and their leaders to walk the walk and talk the talk according to the teachings of the Torah. But the people do not listen. Amos condemns the monarchs who rely on military expertise, and he condemns the priests who make a mockery of worship by merely going through the motions. The entire society is corrupt. God does not want empty, superficial attempts at worship and repentance.

In a lament, the prophet rehearses God's dealing with the people—the times of deliverance and protection—and calls them to repent. Amos challenges the Israelites to get back on track and renew their covenant with God before it's too late. He tells them that their insincere singing and music, their perfunctory participation in festivals and gatherings, their meaningless sacrifices are not acceptable. In fact, those who are most comfortable will be the first to feel God's wrath; for those who are at ease in Zion—just wait, God has a surprise for you:

> Alas for those who lie on beds of ivory,
>   and lounge on their couches,
> and eat lambs from the flock,
>   and calves from the stall;
> who sing idle songs to the sound of the harp,
>   and like David improvise on instruments of music;
> who drink wine from bowls,
>   and anoint themselves with the finest oils,
>   but are not grieved over the ruin of Joseph!

Therefore they shall now be the first to go into exile,
>   and the revelry of the loungers shall pass away.
>   (Amos 6:4–7)

There is very little hope to be found in the book of Amos. The closing verses come closest; God promises to restore the Davidic covenant. Further, God will bring Israel back to glory, but only after the judgment has been fulfilled:

I will restore the fortunes of my people Israel,
>   and they shall rebuild the ruined cities and inhabit them;
> they shall plant vineyards and drink their wine,
>   and they shall make gardens and eat their fruit.
> I will plant them upon their land,
>   and they shall never again be plucked up
>   out of the land that I have given them, says [YHWH] your
>   God.
>   (Amos 9:14–15)

The compassion expressed here leads many scholars to the conclusion that this section is a late addition to the book of Amos. We cannot be certain; however, this closing suits the prophetic work well because it affirms that judgment and restoration are two sides of the same coin.

Amos is important for us today because of his focus on the poor and the oppressed. Of all the prophets, Amos most stimulates our sense of righteous indignation. He heaps the weight of injustice on the shoulders of those in power. He assumes that the wealthy and powerful gain their status by exploiting the less fortunate or by evil, underhanded ways. It is easy to side with Amos because at some point all of us have felt used and abused. We want to believe that Amos speaks for us when he holds the powerful accountable for the plight of the poor.

Amos, however, may be preaching to us, not about us. We in the United States take so many of our privileges for granted—we crave bigger houses, fancier cars, and designer clothes. We go to great lengths to keep up with the Joneses and we pretend that material things bring us happiness, status, and recognition. We desperately try to live the lifestyles of the rich and famous. Yet underneath it all, we experience an emptiness that things cannot fill. When we are honest, we realize that the quality of our relationships often suffer because we are seduced by the notion that bigger is better, that more is best, and the one with the most toys wins.

Amos and God call us to accountability—who suffers so we can live in ease? It is a daunting question and one we must reckon with if we are to live meaningful lives filled with love, peace, and harmony.

REFLECTION QUESTIONS

1. What picture of God emerges in the book of Amos? How does this picture affirm or undermine your experience of God? Explain.

2. Amos preaches during a time of relative peace and stability; how do you think people react to his message?

3. How would you teach or preach a message of justice and righteousness to the rich and powerful of our day? What images would you use to convey your message?

4. Who are the poor and oppressed in our world today? In what ways do you use your privilege against them? What changes do you need to make in order to bring justice to places of oppression?

5. What signs of hope do you see emerging in the world? How can you and/or your faith community support these efforts?

8

Bigotry and Fish

READ:

Jonah 4:1–11

FOCUS TEXT:

[Jonah] prayed to [YHWH] and said, "O [YHWH]!
Is not this what I said while I was still in my own country?
That is why I fled to Tarshish at the beginning; for I knew
that you are a gracious God and merciful, slow to anger, and
abounding in steadfast love, and ready to relent from punishing.
And now, O [YHWH], please take my life from me,
for it is better for me to die than to live."

(Jon. 4:2–3)

Who has not heard of Jonah? Even people most unfamiliar with the
Bible know of the reluctant prophet who is swallowed by the whale.
The story of Jonah reminds us of the Adam and Eve story in
Genesis 3—we think we know the story but are surprised when we
read it. We discover things in the familiar story that aren't there. For
instance, the fruit in Genesis 3 is never identified as an apple—it is

the "fruit" of the tree of the knowledge of good and evil. Likewise, in Jonah, the prophet is swallowed by a large fish; there is no whale in the story. Let's see if there are other discoveries in the book of Jonah.

The book of Jonah is a short book of forty-eight verses, eight of which are poetry (but not prophetic oracles) and the rest prose. The opening verses provide identifying information about the prophet, which is similar to other prophetic works. However, this is where the similarities end. Jonah is an unusual book because it does not follow the protocol of other prophetic works. The book does not contain any prophetic oracles, does not rail against foreign nations or Israel, and does not portray a willing servant in the prophet.

Jonah is identified as the son of Amittai, of whom we know nothing. Jonah is mentioned in 2 Kings 14:25 in the context of Jeroboam II's reign; the prophet helped the monarch in a successful campaign against Syria. Jonah is from Gath-hepher, a Galilean town in the eastern section of land appointed to the tribe of Zebulun (Josh. 19:13). God commands Jonah to go to Nineveh, the capital of Assyria, and prophesy against it. This seems like a reasonable enough command—other prophets are commissioned to preach against cities and nations. How hard can it be?

We have seen reluctance in other prophets—they don't want to rail against their own people; they are intimidated by the nations against which they are to prophesy. But Jonah takes the cake. We know something strange is happening because, following the words of God's commission to Jonah, we read "But." This is always a signal that something out of the ordinary is about to happen—and what a "but" this is. Instead of heading towards Nineveh as commanded, Jonah heads in the opposite direction—towards Tarshish and away from the presence of God! What? What is Jonah thinking and doing here?

Other prophets have resisted the call and the mission but all obeyed, even if they fussed about it the whole time (like Jeremiah). But Jonah outwardly defies God's command. It is not yet clear why

Jonah resists the command. God identifies Nineveh as a "great" city, implying, perhaps, its size, power, and status on the world stage. God injects a sense of urgency—Jonah is to leave immediately on this mission, but Jonah takes his time and makes a decision that puzzles us. He tries to run *away* from God, his call, and his mission. Can he do that? Is this the proper behavior for a prophet of God? What will happen to Jonah for his disobedience and faithlessness? Well, these are only the first of many questions we ask as we explore Jonah's story.

In the first chapter, Jonah is running away from God and keeps going down—down to Tarshish, down to Joppa, down into the bowels of the ship during the storm where he had lain down, he is thrown down into the raging sea, is swallowed down into the belly of a large fish—in his attempt to flee from God, Jonah is on a downward spiral. Each step of his journey takes him deeper and deeper down, but even in the deepest of the deep (the fish's belly), Jonah still cannot escape from the presence of God.

It seems that the only person who does not know this is Jonah. God hurls "a great wind" upon the waters and a ferocious storm ensues. The sailors are afraid, and each prays to his god. They also hurl the cargo overboard, hoping the lightened load will help them right the ship. Some scholars suggest that rather than throwing the wares overboard to lighten the load, the sailors are offering sacrifices to their gods to appease them. At any rate, while the ship is being tossed and driven by a fierce storm, Jonah is sleeping deeply and seems unaware that a storm is even raging. He is roused by the captain, who frantically petitions Jonah to get up and call on his god, who might stop the storm before they all die. Jonah resists the captain's urging just as he has resisted God's urging. Jonah doesn't pray to God and the sailors have to cast lots to determine the cause of the storm—and the culprit is none other than Jonah. The mariners, rightly so, interrogate Jonah: why, what, where, who, seeking information about his job, his origins, and his kinfolk. And Jonah's confession is enough to frighten the sailors (see Jonah 1:9). If Jonah worships the God who made the sea and dry land, he must have done something especially grievous because innocent lives are about to be taken. They ask what they should do with Jonah.

Even at this point, Jonah doesn't pray or petition God—he asks to be thrown overboard. But the sailors, who do not believe in Jonah's God, nevertheless seek to save Jonah and themselves by rowing harder towards land. There is urgency in their motions but their efforts are futile. They don't want to kill Jonah; they want the storm to stop. But they are in a bind—if they don't give up Jonah, they will die. If they do give up Jonah, his God will kill them. They don't know what to do and they resort to the only thing they can—they pray. Only this time, they pray to Jonah's God. These nonbelievers cry out, asking a reprieve from certain death (see Jonah 1:14). The sailors lift up a community complaint prayer that states their innocence and reluctance to kill Jonah.

The sailors are more faithful than Jonah in seeking God's favor. Reluctantly, they hurl Jonah down into the raging sea, which immediately calms down. Jonah refuses to commit suicide but is okay with being murdered! If he is killed, he may finally reach his goal to get away from God. They hurl Jonah overboard and the storm ceases. However, the nonbelieving sailors understand Jonah's God to be the creator of the seas and dry land; they offer sacrifices and vows to Jonah's God. The sailors disappear from the story and Jonah disappears when he is swallowed by a large fish. Jonah takes up residency there for three days and three nights. What's going to happen now? The story is suspenseful and exciting—we can hardly wait to hear what happens next.

We are surprised—in the bowels of the fish, Jonah finally prays to his God. His prayer is earnest and vivid, but it is distorted—read Jonah 2:2–10. Notice that Jonah's prayer is one of thanksgiving, as if he has already been rescued and as if he is in another time and setting. His words don't fit the context of the fish's belly. There is an ongoing scholarly debate about the place and timing for the prayer. Some think this is a late addition to the book; however, not much consensus has been reached. Also note other differences: Jonah cries not from the belly of the fish but rather the belly of Sheol, the underworld place of the dead in the Hebrew Bible (Psa. 115:17); Jonah states that God hurled him into the sea when the sailors did the tossing; Jonah states that God has driven him away when it is Jonah who is fleeing; Jonah is trapped in the sea rather than inside the fish's belly; Jonah is delivered from the Pit (Sheol) rather than the fish's stomach. Jonah is on the verge of death but he thanks God for deliverance. Again, Jonah goes down—see verse 6b. Yet, he claims to be a pious believer who makes the proper sacrifices to God. His prayer does not reflect his actions—he defies God's orders and only when his life is almost gone does he lift up prayers to God for deliverance and salvation.

Is Jonah in denial about his situation? Has he had a change of heart and mind? Does he now see the error of trying to run away from God? Does he understand the difference between worshiping idols and worshiping God? Is Jonah sincere or just trying to save his own hide? If given another chance, will he obey God's commission? Is this prayer all about Jonah with little to do with honoring (or fearing) God? So many questions—where are the answers? The tension and suspense continue to build as we puzzle over Jonah's prayer.

The irony of Jonah's story continues—God orders the fish to swallow Jonah and orders it to spew him out. The sailors and the fish are more obedient to God than Jonah is! But after his prayer and his deliverance, Jonah has another chance to be obedient—what will he do? We can almost hear the exasperation in God's tone as Jonah is commanded, again, to get up and go to Nineveh (3:1–2). This time, Jonah gets up and goes. Jonah travels to the large city of Nineveh and he speaks. His speech is not bracketed with the usual formula for prophetic speech, "Thus says [YHWH] . . ." Jonah does not identify himself to the Ninevites, nor does he qualify his authority to speak. Further, we don't know what God has told Jonah to say. We hear only Jonah's words. His is probably the shortest sermon on record: "Forty days more, and Nineveh shall be overthrown!" (3:4b).

The expression "forty days" usually implies a long period of tribulation (see Exod. 34:27–28; 1 Kings 19:1–8; Ezek. 4:1–6). The English translation "shall be overthrown" is from the Hebrew verb form *nehpāket*, which implies the city will overturn itself. What does Jonah mean here? We cannot be sure. It is not clear if Jonah speaks literally or figuratively. Any long period of time seems inconsistent with the urgency of God's command to Jonah. How can a city overturn itself? Also, it is not clear if the residents of Nineveh know Jonah's God or believe in the deity. What we know from the text is that the people respond! (Does this mean that short sermons can be as powerful as longer ones? ☺) Attention in the narrative now shifts to the people of Nineveh.

The power of Jonah's words is felt throughout the city—the monarch and the people are moved to believe, fast, and pray. They engage in religious practices of fasting, putting on sackcloth (even the animals are covered in sackcloth!), and sitting in ashes. There is no mention of God in Jonah's sermon and yet the people of Nineveh hear, believe, and act. The monarch and the people hope God will have a change of heart and mind and reverse the action against the city. The monarch's actions are decisive: he gets up, takes off his robe, covers himself with sackcloth, and sits in ashes—only then does he proclaim his edict. And no one is exempt, all—human and animal—must get on board. They will not eat or drink water; instead, they will cover themselves with sackcloth, cry to God, and turn from their evil and violent ways. In other ironic words, the city of Nineveh is overturning itself, through a grassroots effort that convinces the monarch to join them! The city repents—it turns away from sin and turns to God. And lo and behold, God turns by changing the divine mind and refusing to destroy the city. The city chooses to overturn itself in the hope that God will let them live; and their actions move God to turn from divine anger and disappointment to a reprieve from the promised destruction.

We would think that this turn of events would make Jonah happy. His short sermon is a resounding success. His few words have saved an entire city. We learn, though, that Jonah is less than pleased. In fact, he is so angry that his reaction puzzles us. Now we learn why Jonah was so bent on running away from his commission in chapter 1 (see Jon. 4:2–3).

Notice how different this prayer is from his last one. There is not a note of thanksgiving here. Instead, Jonah blames God for the positive outcome when Jonah clearly wants to see some destruction. Jonah wants to smell the smoke of flesh and buildings burning. He wants to see people running in chaotic paths with the animals—not people sitting and praying. So disappointed is Jonah that he wants to die. What is up with Jonah and his death wish? Instead of rejoicing at the salvation of Nineveh and taking credit for preaching a right-on sermon, Jonah sulks, pouts, and asks God to kill him. He still refuses to consider suicide, which is a good thing, but he would rather die than rejoice at how God has used him to save an entire city.

God has shown divine mercy and Jonah is angry. God affirms the divine nature—gracious, merciful, slow to anger, abounding in *ḥesed* even for foreigners who do wickedness. But Jonah doesn't care. The city should have been destroyed, and now this? And Jonah pouts and waits to see what will happen to Nineveh. On the one hand, it is refreshing to witness Jonah's deep-down feelings about his work and its outcome; on the other hand, we are distressed at his negative reaction. Jonah wants to see the destruction of the city: he wants the adrenaline rush of smoke, fire, and brimstone; people screaming for their lives and cattle burned to a crisp in an effort to escape the mayhem. But instead, Jonah witnesses the repentance of people who come to believe that Israel's God is, indeed, good, even to the enemies of God's people. And it's all God's fault that the people turned themselves around—what nerve! Both God and the Ninevites are on Jonah's list of folks to rebuke. And after all Jonah has been through—going down to Joppa, fleeing to Tarshish, being thrown into the tempestuous sea, being swallowed whole by a fish, being vomited out by the same fish—all of that was for nothing. Jonah's initial suspicion that God would save Nineveh has come to pass. Wouldn't you be angry, too? How dare God force Jonah to preach to these wicked and violent people—then change the divine mind to spare them! Gee whiz. Imagine Jonah sitting all alone in his misery. Is there no satisfying him?

When God speaks, God does not engage Jonah on his level of accusation. God does not remind Jonah how he was saved from a watery death. God does not recite the divine mercy and grace extended to Jonah while in the fish's belly. God asks what we are asking, "Dude! What is up with you? Why are you angry? The outcome is a good one." Jonah is done with God—he goes out, sits down just outside the city, makes a booth for himself, and sits in the shade—never mumbling a word. Until God kills him, all Jonah can do is sit. And so he sits . . . and sits . . . and sits.

The book of Jonah closes on a somber note and unanswered question. God's actions toward Jonah serve as an object lesson for the unhappy prophet. A plant is "appointed" by God to shade Jonah from the burning heat of the sun—the bushy plant makes Jonah happy. Since it's all about Jonah, he doesn't complain about God's mercy and graciousness in providing additional shade. Jonah's anger has turned to joy and delight. But the next morning, God "appoints" a worm to eat the plant so it withers. After sunrise, God "appoints" an east wind that is hot and exacerbates the heat of the sun on Jonah. These movements are God's doing. Perhaps God is giving Jonah a chance to overturn himself—to help Jonah move from anger to joy, from bigoted resentment to radical inclusivity, from bitterness to love.

When the plant withers and his shade is gone, Jonah turns back to anger. Since it's all about Jonah, he wishes to die because of his discomfort (see 4:8). This is the third time he expresses the desire to die—when will God heed his words? Instead, God poses another question to Jonah—is he more concerned about a bush than a people? If he is, Jonah is not a fitting prophet. Jonah does not answer and the book ends. Jonah does not display compassion for the people of Nineveh but does for the withered plant; is his concern for the plant itself or for the lack of shade it provides him? We've known Jonah to be a self-interested and reluctant missionary. We would not be surprised if his emotion is related to his own lack rather than for the life of the plant. He replies as he has in the past—he is angry enough to die. So much emotion for a plant and none for humans and animals. God is not pleased and lets the divine inquiry hang over Jonah's head and ours.

Scholars are divided about how to interpret the Jonah story. Most agree that the narrative has less to do with the historical Jonah and more with the lessons to be gleaned from it. Some suggest that the book is a parody that caricatures a "false" prophet—the reluctant messenger who does all he can to avoid his divine commission. It is clear that the book is filled with irony—Jonah's futile attempt to run from God; the sailors' uncritical and quick belief in God and their willingness to sacrifice and make vows to the deity; the large fish swallowing and vomiting out Jonah; the quick response of Nineveh to Jonah's short sermon; Jonah's unexplained anger about the fate of Nineveh; Jonah's obsessive concern for a plant. The story does not imply that one should not care about plants; the story highlights Jonah's lack of compassion for human and animal life. His concern should be balanced and it is not. Some believe that the book was composed after the fall of Israel and Judah—if this is the case, Jonah has good reason to be resentful. God saves Nineveh but lets Israel and Judah perish. The interpretation of the book of Jonah remains open.

As a prophetic work, there are some things to explore further. One is whether we can ignore God's call and commission. We may not want to do what God tells us to do; Jonah certainly didn't. God does not force Jonah, but allows him to undergo a series of events. It is up to Jonah to interpret them and decide on his course of action. In dramatic form, God gives Jonah the freedom to choose. Now we may feel that Jonah doesn't really have a choice—he is thrown overboard and swallowed by a fish. He gives in to God's will and is upset when his words are efficacious. He pouts and sulks when God refuses to destroy the city. Does Jonah really have free will?

Secondly, Jonah does not mask his anger. And his anger neither moves God to change the divine decision about Nineveh or about the plant. God does not tell Jonah he should not be angry—anger is a legitimate emotion and Jonah is free to express his feelings. God does not engage Jonah on the level of anger; Jonah feels the way he does and so does God. In this narrative, we learn that we are free to express the rawest of feelings—our emotions do not diminish God nor do they affect our relationship with God. There are some things for which we should be angry; God poses to Jonah (and to us) just what should arouse anger and what should be accepted as the way things are. God, too, expresses anger in the narrative.

Thirdly, we often overlook the grassroots efforts of the Ninevites. Before the monarch even knows that Jonah has preached doom for the city, the people organize themselves and take action. This is certainly a lesson for all of us. We can wait for our leaders to set policies and practices, but the efforts of the people can affect the systems that rule over all of us. Certainly the U.S. civil rights movement prompted by African Americans in the South set the standard for holding the government accountable for the well-being of its citizens. We must not underestimate the power of the poor black men, women, and children who brought conscious intention to bear on the policies of the United States during the 1940s, 1950s, and

1960s. Blacks and their sympathizers put their lives on the line for freedom, justice, and protection under the law. They served as models for other liberation movements in the United States, including equal rights for women, Native American Indians, gays and lesbians—and the list continues. Grassroots movements are powerful and are often light years ahead of what politicians and other leaders may think is prudent.

Fourthly, the book of Jonah helps us get a glimpse of God's radical inclusivity based in an understanding of justice. The enemy of God's people is saved from destruction. If God can have mercy on Nineveh, God can have mercy on anyone God chooses. For those who repent (overturn themselves), there is hope of salvation, redemption, and deliverance. Justice can prevail for those who correct their behavior to reflect justice. Now, we might question God's concern for the plant that is attacked by a worm. But whether sea, wind, plant, worm, or Ninevites—God is in charge of the cosmos. Jonah declares that God is the Creator of the seas and dry land; we can add the universe to this list. God is able to do what God wants and wills for the universe and cosmos. We may question God's choices and we might not like the divine decisions, but ultimately it is God's choice. We trust and believe that God brings shalom to the land and to the cosmos.

REFLECTION QUESTIONS

1. Have you ever tried to run away from God? What were the reasons for your resistance? What was the outcome of your efforts?

2. How do you deal with anger? Do these methods work for you? Explain.

3. What issues should evoke righteous indignation? What can you do about these issues and concerns? What keeps you from doing more?

4. What picture of God emerges in the book of Jonah? How do you feel about how God deals with Jonah?

5. How is justice implied in the book of Jonah? In what ways is Jonah a prophetic work? How does this book defy your understanding of prophetic books?

9

Living, Doing, and Traveling

READ:

Micah 6:6–8

FOCUS TEXT:

[God] has told you, O mortal, what is good; and what does [YHWH] require of you but to do justice, and to love kindness, and to walk humbly with your God?

(Mic. 6:8)

If we thought Amos was harsh and unrelenting, we haven't seen anything until we explore Micah's message. We would think that tough words would be nuanced and that the prophet would find ways to finesse his message so that people would not be turned off; however, Micah doesn't seem to care whether folks are put off by his message. Instead, Micah is a feisty advocate for the poor and paints explicit pictures of their oppression and exploitation. The prophetic poet from Moresheth is one of the common folk. He does not have the status that allows him audiences with the monarch or other persons in power. Instead, he identifies with the poor and the oppressed, who are innocent victims of those in power. Yes, he calls out the leaders of his day—with power and authority.

In fact, he seems to relish shocking his listeners. But when we read between the lines, we find that Micah, too, smarts from the message he preaches. It is clear that Micah is part of the community to which he preaches. He stands under the judgment of God along with others in his audience. His message hurts, and he experiences the pain of his community. His call to justice involves not simply the public life of politicians and religious leaders but also the private lives of visible leaders and everyday people. Micah is the prosecuting voice in God's lawsuit against Israel and Judah—and there's no way God loses this case.

Micah gives us the much loved passage in chapter 6—you have probably heard dozens of sermons on the text. We will unpack this passage and set it in the context of Micah's time. At least, we will try. The book of Micah is relatively short but is filled with many confusing elements: there are awkward transitions, unexpected changes from judgment and condemnation to promise and hope, and sudden shifts in personal pronouns and gender. It is not easy to follow Micah; but, the bottom line is clear—God judges Judah because of the unjust practices of its leaders, all must suffer, even the innocent, but God will redeem the people and the land.

Micah prophesies during the reigns of Jotham, Ahaz, and Hezekiah in Judah. The northern nation, Israel, is captured by the Assyrians with the rise to power of Tiglath-pileser III in 746 B.C.E. Although Israel has enjoyed a time of prosperity, its fortunes turn with the death of Jeroboam II. Israel falls to Assyria and Judah gets a short reprieve. Judah is not left unscathed. It becomes a vassal state to Assyria and is forced to pay tributes (taxes) to Assyria. In the face of a political threat, Judah begins its own internal decline into idolatry and corruption. For Micah and other prophets, the fate of Israel foreshadows what is to come for Judah, if the people don't change.

The book of Micah begins with an opening argument in God's lawsuit against Israel and its capital city Samaria. God's judgment against Israel is clear—Samaria is no longer a city, but barren fields; its idols are smashed and destroyed; it sells itself (prostitutes) to foreign nations. It cannot stand as an independent state any longer (see Mic. 1:6–7).

Israel is seen as the wayward child after it seceded from the united monarchy under David's leadership. Israel's rebellion is seen as not one against the monarchy but rather one against God; its life is marked by idolatry and infidelity to the covenantal responsibilities. There is no hope for the nation because it has strayed from its roots and tradition. The march of Assyria against Israel is "proof" that it has set its own course toward destruction. The prophet warns that Judah, too, is on that same path of annihilation.

The people believe that they can do anything they want because God promised an eternal dynasty to David's family; that is, there will always be a descendant of David in charge in Judah. Further, the people believe that Judah will always stand as an independent nation because God dwells in the capital city of Jerusalem. Surely, God will not let anyone or anything destroy the divine residence. The people and their leaders live with arrogance and believe their transgressions will be forgiven, that God will never forsake them.

Micah warns them that their false sense of security will be their undoing. Although Micah is not from Jerusalem, he laments its fate. Moresheth is a small village southwest of Jerusalem about twenty-five miles away. Many prophets use laments in their messages to convey their own sense of dread and pain at impending threats and disasters. Through laments, the prophet embodies the distress of events or impending events. Micah's pain is so deep that he expresses his despair by going barefoot and naked and by weeping and wailing uncontrollably. His language is graphic and carries a sense of urgency:

For this I will lament and wail;
    I will go barefoot and naked;
I will make lamentation like the jackals,
    and mourning like the ostriches.
For her wound is incurable.
    It has come to Judah;
it has reached to the gate of my people,
    to Jerusalem.
    (Mic. 1:8–9)

Micah believes that Judah is on the downward spiral because of the "sins" of the leaders—those charged with protecting the population and with ensuring that justice is the rule of the day. Micah indicts the monarchs and the wealthy who stay up all night coming up with plans to wreak havoc in the nation—they take lands that don't belong to them and to which they have no moral right; they subvert the law to cover their dastardly plans; they oppress the less fortunate without remorse (see Mic. 2:1–2). God says that their deeds do not go unpunished and what they are doing to others will be done to them: they will lose everything, including their dignity and wealth.

The Israelites believe that they are stewards of the land that ultimately belongs to God. The land is given so that each household can sustain itself. The sustenance of an agrarian lifestyle depends on good seed, good soil, good weather, and good harvests. A disruption in any of these factors leads to poverty. It is then the responsibility of the community to help out until things are balanced. With the monarchy and the movement to urban centers, farmers are required to turn more and more of their proceeds over to the government. There are fewer resources to help farmers in lean years; if there is a bad harvest, the farmer must still pay taxes to the government. Wealthy landowners make loans to struggling farmers, using the land as collateral. The poor farmer gets deeper and deeper in debt until the wealthy landowners are able to take the land outright. Women and children are left homeless and penniless. Such usurpation of land is sinful in Israel, but that does not stop unscrupulous landowners and developers from taking advantage of their fellow citizens. To these greedy hoarders of land Micah speaks.

And Micah is warned by other prophets to tone down his message. In fact, they tell him to shut up (see Mic. 2:6). They wrongly believe that nothing of what Micah says can happen. They live in denial, confident that God will always forgive them and keep them safe from danger. Micah rejects their advice and goes on with his message; he even chastises them for telling lies to the people (see Mic. 3:5–7). None of them will receive a word, vision, direction, or signal from God—if they ever did. They have nothing to commend them to the people because they are not sent by God. Micah declares his power and authority as a true prophet of God. Micah doesn't claim that he alone is worthy, but rather that God has chosen and empowered him to prophesy (see Mic. 3:8).

Micah reframes the prophetic office for his listeners. The job of the prophet is not to soften a harsh message or give in to the wishes of the elite and powerful. The job of the prophet is to speak the truth, no matter how difficult and no matter how uncomfortable it makes those who hear it. Micah exercises his office because he is filled with God's Spirit and power, God's justice and might—not for his own gain, but as a mouthpiece for God. His work is authentic because he speaks for God.

But the false prophets are not the only ones deceiving the people. The very leaders who should be protecting the people and ensuring their rights are the ones who are ravaging them instead; they are no better than cannibals. The politicians and other leaders conspire together to oppress the people (see Mic. 3:1–3).

Micah pulls no punches in his indictment of those charged with dispensing justice. Micah uses hyperbole to get his message across so there is no misunderstanding. What the leaders do is abominable and is not to be excused or softened. They are devouring the innocent and they will pay for their crimes. But it is not just the rich and powerful who will pay—everyone suffers for the sins of the few. The innocent, the oppressed, and the exploited, too, will go through trials and tribulations. The entire community comes under indictment, starting with the rulers, priests, and prophets. Those responsible for the coming doom represent all aspects of public life: the leaders, the priests, and even the prophets pervert justice (read Mic. 3:9–11).

It is not clear what Micah refers to when he says, "Zion is built with blood and Jerusalem with wrong." He may be lifting up the ambivalence about the monarchy always at work even during David's golden years of leadership and the extreme measures of the government under Solomon, who imposed forced labor and heavy taxes for his building projects. At any rate, Jerusalem is corrupt through and through, and no good end is possible. The safety net the people have depended upon is gone—they live in denial if they think their crimes will go unpunished. Micah warns them that because the head is sick, the body will suffer. For Micah, there is no easy way out—devastation and destruction are necessary consequences for the failures of Judah's leadership.

For many, especially those in power, Micah prophesies the impossible. There is no way God is going to abandon the favored people and the favored city. No wonder the other prophets tell Micah to sit down and be quiet. Their hopes hang on a God who promises never to leave or abandon them. Even though Israel has fallen, Judah will never fall. Micah will be proven wrong, the people say.

Then Micah gives a mixed message. On the one hand, destruction is inevitable. The sins and covenant violations are too numerous and too deep. Get ready, for the end is coming, Micah warns. On the other hand, Micah speaks of God's restoration—a time when Jerusalem will regain its former glory and all the nations will know that God does, indeed, prevail over the evil of the chosen nation and all other nations. Peace and prosperity will once again be the order of the day: swords will be beaten into plowshares and spears into pruning hooks, and nations will study war no more (read Mic. 4:2b–3).

Judah will no longer be the laughingstock on the world stage. God will be vindicated and the people redeemed. Hope is possible despite the suffering that must occur. Micah does not leave the people hopeless—they will go "through" the valley of despair and destruction but they will not remain there. The ultimate word of God is hope—there is a future because God keeps divine promises even when the people must endure the consequences of their decisions and choices. In fact, Micah speaks of a messiah who comes from Bethlehem, the site of David's appointment (see 1 Sam. 16). This reference connects with God's choice of the humble and God's covenant with David for an eternal dynasty. God will raise up a ruler who is committed to justice, righteousness, and truth (see Mic. 5:3–5).

The new ruler will not be corrupt or weak; this one will keep covenantal obligations and lead the people in caring, compassionate, and healthy ways. The new ruler will make sure that social, religious, and economic policies and practices are in line with God's intention for community and national life—serving as prime examples of what God's realm is truly about with a commitment to the common good. The new ruler of God's choosing is not specifically identified as a "messiah," although messianic elements are obvious.

In contrast to his scathing indictment of the leaders and the people of Judah, Micah ultimately returns to a message of hope. All will be okay in the end. And he leaves only the lingering question of what God expects from the people in return for God's justice and mercy.

This brings us to the focus text for this study, Micah 6. After a series of twists and turns, the downs of judgment and the ups of hope, Micah states that God requires a lifestyle change. The chapter opens with God's lawsuit against Israel, a case that is continuing. God's testimony is that the people have been saved over and over again and all the earth knows it. God rehearses the Exodus story, the centerpiece of divine intervention and deliverance. And instead of living lives as a people intimately aware of God's love and justice, the people engage in empty religious ceremonies. However, it is not enough to perform rituals and religious rites. These become perfunctory and lose all meaning. The purposes behind the rituals are lost and people go through the motions. Leaders fall back on rituals to excuse their unjust behaviors and motivations. People think they can erase their crimes by putting on a show of righteousness and right behavior. Micah states clearly that these shams do not fool God. God is looking for genuine people, not pretenders.

On the surface, what God requires seems simple. But living into these expectations is anything but. Micah lays out a threefold lifestyle plan:

1. To do justice: the Hebrew word, *mišpāṭ*, conveys both righting old wrongs and engaging in practices based on fair and equitable principles. God asks the people to *do* justice—not just when it is expedient but always as the standard of relating to each other. Doing justice is the only way to live out the covenant responsibility; this justice is God's intention for the whole created order and governs every aspect of life so that fairness and impartiality rules.

2. To love kindness: the Hebrew word, *ḥesed*, is a covenant concept that is difficult to translate into English. The word implies everlasting love and care. God has *ḥesed* for us and we are to have *ḥesed* for each other. God and people are bound together in solidarity and live in steadfast loyalty to God and to other human beings. The concept embraces intimacy, trust, loyalty, and fidelity.

3. To walk humbly with God: the Hebrew word, *hālak*, is modified by the adjective "humbly" (Hebrew *ṣn'*)—we are to walk with God by putting God at the center of our lives. We live as people who know, love, and appreciate God as creator, redeemer, and sustainer. To walk humbly means we live according to God's instructions and intentions for creation.

Therefore, those who don't adopt this lifestyle get what they deserve—judgment and despair. They leave God no choice but to bring the judgment that will ultimately make things right again. In other words, the people have to live out the consequences of their choices so that peace, harmony, and equilibrium are achieved. The consequences are clear:

> Therefore I have begun to strike you down,
>> making you desolate because of your sins.
> You shall eat, but not be satisfied,
>> and there shall be a gnawing hunger within you;
> you shall put away, but not save,
>> and what you save, I will hand over to the sword.
> You shall sow, but not reap;
>> you shall tread olives, but not anoint yourselves with oil;
>> you shall tread grapes, but not drink wine.
> (Mic. 6:13–15)

Whatever people expect to gain by deceit, lies, and trickery will be lost in the end. The book of Micah ends with a dramatic lament that contains deep anguish and prophetic hope. Both God and Micah mourn the stubbornness of God's people. Micah reiterates his trust in God and God's ways. Micah pleads with God to be true to God's nature of compassion and fidelity. Far from flattering God, Micah's prayer is filled with pain and trust in the midst of a tough time: God pardons iniquity, passes over transgressions, and will overcome divine anger and have compassion on God's people. In fact, sins will be cast into the sea and forgotten (read Mic. 7:18–20).

Through it all, Micah declares, God will be God. Micah is a prophet who batters us back and forth between judgment and mercy. God is a violent stickler for details one minute, and a gentle shepherd the next. Micah's God seems schizophrenic in the ways in which the deity interacts with humans. Yet the message of Micah does not differ from the other prophets in the Hebrew Bible—if we refuse to turn back to God and away from our sins of injustice and exploitation, we will get what we deserve.

Micah raises all kinds of questions about the nature of God and the issue of theodicy, or why the righteous suffer. The questions we raise are rooted in our Christian heritage that portrays God as kind, loving, and ever patient. Because of Jesus, we understand God to be one who means to bring a new world order. The prophets confirm, however, that both portraits of God are accurate.

There is only one God. That one God does marvelous things and intervenes into the concrete history of our lives. At the same time, this God intends for justice and peace to be the center of public and private life. We cannot do whatever we want and disregard the consequences. We are held accountable to God and to each other for the choices and decisions we make. Our actions mean something and we cannot cover them up with empty rituals and ceremonies. God means for the created order to live shalom—not just the absence of war but also the well-being of all creation.

The greed and immoral practices of the United States are being exposed in the early decade of the twenty-first century. The economic and military crises do not spring from nothing—they uncover illegal and immoral activities at the highest levels of leadership. The hunger for power and wealth manifests in the exploitation and abuse of people who seek only a better life for themselves and their children.

The "bailout" of businesses—too big to be allowed to fail—ought to result in a resetting of priorities and what constitutes the good life. Profits are not unlimited; greed must be contained; the vulnerable must be protected. It does not take a crystal ball to see what happens when there are no checks and balances in government, business, or church. God holds us to a higher standard.

The declaration of war on small nations and the military occupation of many more do not make for peace. The undermining of sovereign nations so the United States can export their natural resources that fuel the extravagant lifestyles of a few will not go unaccounted for; someone will pay. Even by conservative counts, the United States has a military presence in more than 70 percent of the world's countries and in places most U.S. citizens have never heard of (visit http://www.lewrockwell.com for some insights). Under the guise of "the war on terrorism," the United States justifies its military and corporate presence around the globe and is not held accountable by anyone, not even its own citizenry. This network of power and intimidation leaves smaller countries without options and their people devastated. Despite rebellions and resistance by indigenous people and governments, the United States exerts its power and gets its way even if it means destroying the land.

Sooner or later, the bill will become due. Micah warns us that we cannot bury our heads in the sand and pretend that all is right with the world. We, too, live in the tension between judgment and hope, lament and faith. The world is a mess—war and violence, poverty and fear, political and corporate corruption, racism and homophobia abound and are pervasive throughout the world.

Micah exercises his freedom of speech and critiques the social scene of his time. His words continue to ring true for us—the only way out is a total change, a turn from self-interests and a turn to God. And what is required of us? The formula has not changed: to do justice, love kindness, and walk humbly with our God. We have no excuses; the plight of Israel and Judah is our wake-up call.

REFLECTION QUESTIONS

1. Summarize Micah's message about justice and community. Given your social location and context, what would you add to his message? What would you change about his message?

2. How do you define power? In what ways do you exercise power? In what ways are you powerless?

3. Make a list of social, economic, political, and religious privileges you enjoy. Who suffers so you can exercise your privileges? What can you do about this?

4. Name three ways you can become better informed about U.S. practices at home and across the globe. Remember that mainstream media serve the interest of those in power.

5. Over what should we offer lament today? How can we instill hope for those who cannot see the way out of despair?

10

Writing on the Wall

READ:

Habakkuk 2:1–3

FOCUS TEXT:

Then [YHWH] answered me and said:
Write the vision; make it plain on tablets,
so that a runner may read it.

(Hab. 2:2)

We don't know anything about Habakkuk except that he is identified as a prophet in the opening verse of the book. His message focuses on one issue: why a just God allows injustice to prevail. The book is shaped around two debates between prophet and God and a closing prayer. Like other prophets, Habakkuk is keenly concerned with issues of justice on both a national and international scale.

It is believed that the prophet lived during the reign of Jehoiakim, which makes him a contemporary of Jeremiah's. Both prophets live during the time when Assyria is being supplanted as a superpower by the Medes and the Chaldeans, who later become the

leaders of Babylonia. After Josiah is killed by Neco of Egypt in 609
B.C.E., Jehoahaz becomes monarch of Judah, but he is succeeded by
Jehoiakim (see 2 Kings 23:34–24:6). After the Egyptians are de-
feated in 605 by the Babylonians, Jehoiakim switches allegiance to
Nebuchadnezzar. In an attempt to bring independence back to
Judah, Jehoiakim rebels against the Babylonians, he is killed, and
Jerusalem is taken.

Scholars have compared the book of Habakkuk to Job and the
Psalms because all deal with the issue of theodicy. Theodicy deals
with the meaning of undeserved suffering before a silent or passive
God. In the first debate with God, Habakkuk sets the stage: there
is wickedness and injustice within Judah, but where is God?
Habakkuk's emotions are right on the surface; in desperation he
asks, "how long," "why," "where are you?" (read Hab. 1:2–4). The
prophet feels that God is silent or absent—how else could the injustice he sees go unpunished? Furthermore, the prophet doesn't
understand why God makes him so sensitive to injustice (see 1:3).

Others seem oblivious to the shenanigans around them, but
not Habakkuk. For him, justice is perverted ('āqal, meaning
"twisted" or "bent")—he speaks of violence, wrongdoing, trouble,
destruction, strife, contention. In dramatic terms, he states that
"justice never prevails." Habakkuk is sickened by what he sees happening in his nation. The poor leadership of Jehoiakim is docu-
mented in 2 Kings and by the prophet Jeremiah. Jehoiakim is accused of forcing the poor into free labor for his building campaigns
and imposing heavy taxes in order to pay his tribute to Egypt and
later Babylonia. The Judean monarch is also accused of influencing
trials and murdering God's prophets (see Jer. 22:13; 22:17;
26:20–23). Throughout Judah, Habakkuk witnesses the unfair accumulation of wealth at the expense of the poor, the oppression of
the less fortunate, the use of loopholes to get away with injustice.
The "righteous" are surrounded by the "wicked" and justice is not
possible. Things are bad and getting worse, Habakkuk says. And he

dares to ask God why these things are happening. Habakkuk critiques the national scene in Judah—things are bad and God is doing nothing about it.

God doesn't respond directly to Habakkuk's charges. Instead, God sets forth the divine plan—God will use the Chaldeans to punish Judah. God describes the Chaldeans in vivid terms: fierce, impetuous, dreadful, fearless, ravaging, and violent. They are like fearless predators that no one, not even Judah, can resist (read Hab. 1:6–11). They will be God's instrument in teaching Judah a lesson. Although God does not explicitly state that the Chaldeans are being used to judge Judah, such is implied in the Hebrew use of plural forms for "look" and "see" in verse 5. God is not talking only to Habakkuk but rather to all of Judah. The work God refers to is the divine response to the injustices in Judah. God is allowing Judah to fall into the hands of its enemy because of its internal refusal to deal justly with its citizens.

The Chaldeans are a force with which to reckon: their might is like a god to them; they are strong, well equipped, and able to subdue any challenge. They represent imperial power on the prowl to expand its borders by any means necessary. Habakkuk, along with other prophets, believes that God is in charge of the universe. Thus, God is in control of history, even those who are not believers. So it is assumed that the coming invasion is part of God's plan to deal with Judah—Judah will get what it deserves because of its disobedience to covenant responsibilities that include communal life and justice. But the violence of the coming Chaldeans will result in a good end—Judah will learn a lesson and turn back to God.

For Habakkuk, God's plan has merits. But he still has issues with God. Habakkuk holds the belief that God is good and holy:

> Your eyes are too pure to behold evil,
>   and you cannot look on wrongdoing;
> why do you look on the treacherous,

and are silent when the wicked swallow
those more righteous than they?
(Hab. 1:13)

Habakkuk's second debate with God focuses on the ruthlessness of
the Chaldeans. Why is God using a people known for unfair war
tactics to teach Judah a lesson? Habakkuk believes that God should
not use a bad nation to teach a bad nation a lesson. The Chaldeans
are corrupt and greedy; they use their might to expand their territory and their power and influence. The Babylonians exhibit the
characteristics of ancient Near East empires—formidable military
weaponry and tactics, great wealth from tributes assessed to conquered territories, and no compassion or concern for the indigenous
peoples captured. Those captured are like fish—hooked, dragged in
nets, gathered up, and killed—destroyed for the sport of it. This is
life under the empire.

It is likely that Habakkuk is an eyewitness to the oppression of
the Chaldeans—after Jehoiakim dies, his son succeeds him.
Jehoiachin is deported by the Babylonians. Zedekiah, the last
monarch of Judah, is enthroned as a vassal to the Babylonian
Empire. Under the empire, Habakkuk witnesses a whole new set of
injustices. Things have gone from bad to worse, indeed. Instead of
bringing peace and justice, the Babylonians bring their own brand
of oppression. God's plan is not working. One corrupt government
has been replaced by another corrupt government and neither
works well for the common folk. And still God does nothing.

Habakkuk critiques the state of the world and God's unwillingness to do anything about it. Habakkuk does not question God's
power or capacity; he wonders why God is not moving more decisively on the side of the oppressed and marginalized. God again does
not respond directly to Habakkuk. God assures the prophet that
things are moving according to plan. And Habakkuk's job is to help
others hang on until God's plan is fulfilled. God means to bring jus-

tice to the land, in God's own time, and in God's own way. There is a way to peace, justice, and prosperity for all—just wait for it.

Habakkuk is told to write the vision—plainly and large enough for all to see, even if they are on the run! Take the message to the streets that God yet reigns and all the ills of society will be fixed at God's appointed time. It appears that the wicked are in control, but the reality is that they will answer for their crimes. The righteous, the oppressed, the marginalized will be vindicated. Ultimately, good will win over evil—just hang in there until it happens. As God does with other prophets, God does not give the specifics but asks for patience. This patience is not a passive waiting but rather one grounded in the belief that God will keep divine promises of well-being for all of creation.

In Habakkuk 2:5–20, there is a shift. The nations that have been oppressed break their silence and speak up. They state that justice will prevail because wickedness and oppression will not last forever. This speech addresses issues of wealth accumulation, the need for safety and longevity, the use of violence, the desire for glory and status, and the worship of idols. And for each offense, there is a reversal for the oppressor; that which the empire seeks will turn on it. Instead of pride and honor, the oppressor will be mocked, taunted, and shamed. The power of the empire is not permanent; indeed, history bears this out. Empires rise and fall—none endure, not even Judah and Israel. Inevitably, the very nature of imperialism precludes endurance and longevity. Ill-gotten gains will, by necessity, be undone. There is a sense in which the rise of the empire is also the beginning of its downfall—ruthless tactics, senseless violence, disregard for life are not sustainable over the long haul. The ways of the empire breed rebellion and resistance—sooner or later, all empires fall. It's the way of the world, God reminds Habakkuk and us.

The book ends with a prayer highlighting God's ultimate power over empires and the cosmos. God is portrayed as a divine warrior bringing justice and equity to the land. Today, we are reluctant to think about God in warrior ways. But God is different from human warriors who wreak havoc for imperialist reasons. Human warriors kill and plunder because they are greedy and power hungry. God as divine warrior engages in warlike behavior to right wrongs and to bring justice to unjust situations. God fights to save people; Habakkuk believes God will ride in on a stallion and once again save God's people. Human armies are fierce, but God is fiercer. What's more, no matter how bad things are politically, socially, and economically, God is still in control of God's world. No matter that there is famine and drought and deprivation in the land; God still reigns in the cosmos. Nothing and no one is more powerful than God.

The power of the book of Habakkuk remains. There are national issues in the United States crying out for redress: failing systems in health care, education, and welfare; crumbling infrastructures, including bridges, levees, dams, and roads; underfunding for the arts; the demise of small family farms; the ever-growing prison industrial complex that disproportionately criminalizes people of color; historical and ongoing oppression of and discrimination against African Americans, Native American Indians, the Chinese, the Japanese, and Hispanics; uneven immigration protocols and racial profiling; the quest for national security that targets Muslims and persons of Arab descent; ongoing bailouts for corporations and big business at the expense of the common good. The list goes on. The people are suffering and dying. Where is God?

There are international issues grounded in U.S. hegemony that cry out for redress: U.S. global militarization; use of torture; the murder of innocent civilians in Afghanistan, Pakistan, and Iraq; the undermining of sovereign governments in the Middle East, Africa, and the Caribbean; a lack of humanitarian aid for HIV/AIDS and poverty; a lack of food and shelter for displaced persons; the disregard for Palestinian freedom and the uncritical support of Israeli war crimes. In lands across the globe, the United States is seen as empire—apparent or in the making. Our military presence in nations is not always benign. Our hands are covered with the blood of innocent people. U.S. citizens need to become more informed about U.S. activities around the world—in Haiti, the Sudan, Kosovo, Cuba, and other places. The list goes on. The people are suffering and dying. Where is God?

The vision that Habakkuk is compelled to write is not explicitly stated in the text. Perhaps the vision is different for each slice of history. The details will differ, but the message remains the same: God reigns. What that means for each generation is for God's people to outline. We have a lot of outlining to do on the national and international fronts. We must become more informed and we must support organizations and agencies that bring life rather than death. In this age of increasing secularism, in this time when people declare themselves "spiritual but not religious," in this era when the religious right with its narrow dispassionate nationalistic agenda sets public policies, in this slice of time when compassion and community are disappearing—we need a revival, a dramatic reminder of God's presence and power.

We pray with Habakkuk and plainly write the vision that peace, harmony, love, and justice will prevail—that God reigns and ultimately will bring to fulfillment the shalom for which we hunger and thirst. We give voice to Habakkuk's plea:

> O [YHWH], I have heard of your renown,
> and I stand in awe, O [YHWH], of your work.
> In our own time revive it;
> in our own time make it known;
> in wrath may you remember mercy.
> (Hab. 3:2)

REFLECTION QUESTIONS

1. How do you define righteousness? How do you define evil? How does the church respond to these theological categories?

2. Habakkuk, Job, the psalmist, and Jeremiah ask why the righteous suffer at the hands of the wicked. Who in your community is suffering and who is prospering? What is the cause for the gap between the two?

3. In what ways does the United States display imperialistic characteristics? What can the ordinary citizen do to hold the government accountable for actions in the United States and across the globe? What are you willing to do to bring justice to the globe?

4. What are the ecological and environmental concerns the church, the community, and the nation should be addressing? What are you willing to do about these issues?

5. Have you ever been angry with God? How did you deal with your anger?

Suggestions for Preaching and Teaching the Hebrew Prophets

<hr/>

The prophets of the Hebrew Bible deal with oppression—those who oppress and those who are oppressed—and God's response to the oppressed and to the oppressor. The "stories" of the prophets are not easy to teach or preach. There is a tendency to be all doom and gloom or to focus on redemption without adequately dealing with God's anger and judgment. It is important to understand that God's "judgment and wrath" stem from the divine sense of justice—some things require righteous indignation. God's judgment is not about satisfying the divine ego; instead it is about setting things right, bringing shalom out of values distortion and breaches in community. The voices of the prophets can be harsh to hear and we are tempted to become defensive or frightened. The teaching and preaching task is to hold both God's judgment and God's love in creative tension. We are moved to repent (to turn from what is distorted) and to re-turn to God in praise, worship, and love. Clearly, the prophets had to deal with this tension and we are not exempt from that struggle.

As we consider teaching and preaching the prophets, we must shift our vision from our comfort in "Zion" to that of the widow, orphan, and stranger. The economic meltdown in the United States and around the globe in these early years of the twenty-first century helps us to move from the comfort zone to one that tests our faith and belief that things will always be good for us. For the first time in a long time, persons with good jobs are worried about the future—their retirement funds are dwindling; they owe more for their homes than they are worth; credit is more difficult to obtain; they are not able to save enough to send their children to college—the list goes on. How surprising to learn that this new reality is an old reality for masses of women, men, and children—in this country and around the globe. While we fret over our credit scores, whole towns and villages are dying because there is no clean water. While we grunt over the rising prices of oil and gasoline, whole nations are waging war against formidable enemies while civilians are indiscriminately slaughtered. The Hebrew prophets challenge us to rethink our priorities and name where we are complicit with the oppression of others here at home and across the globe.

The lessons of the prophets are not easy or fun—but they are necessary if we wish to claim our kinship as children of God. What affects one branch of the family affects us all. We are connected to each other—oppressor and oppressed. Even those who claim oppressed status can be oppressor in certain situations. We must acknowledge those places of privilege and work to live conscious lives—concerned for our sisters and brothers by making responsible choices and decisions and by being critical of our leaders who are supposed to represent our interests and values.

The Hebrew prophets present some of the most challenging opportunities for teaching and preaching. There are not many familiar "stories" to draw on; instead, we are confronted with oracles and proclamations of destruction and impending doom—not happy episodes, to be sure. The challenge should not deter us from trying to bring the prophets into the twenty-first century. Now that we have had the opportunity to explore some passages from the prophetic literature of the Bible, how do we go about the task of teaching them? Are there ways we can move beyond the superficial and stereotypical to explore their deeper meanings and lessons for us today? There is so much gore and blood in these texts that it is easier to ignore them. All of the passages have something to teach us—about valor, courage, creativity, faithfulness, obedience, and love as well as about egotism, selfishness, fear, deception, doubt, and despair—for we move in and out of these stances.

TEACHING

The following teaching ideas can be interchanged among the prophetic texts and should be attempted after studying the appropriate unit in the book. The exercises are designed to answer the following seven questions:

1. Who are the "characters" in the text?

2. What is the action of the text?

3. What is the leadership and/or moral challenge presented in the story?

4. Who speaks and who is silent? What do these actions mean?

5. What do we feel and think as we interact with the text?

6. How is the challenge resolved? What other questions are raised by the text?

7. What can we learn about justice, mission, and ministry as well about ourselves from the text?

I hope that these texts will inspire, encourage, and challenge us. How can we read these passages to explore our own privilege, issues, and concerns? How do we use these passages to delve deeper into who we are as children of God and disciples of Christ? How can these passages deepen our commitment to serve God and humanity through our leadership, ministry, and mission? What can we take from these stories that will help us along our journeys?

Suggested activities include the following:

- Compose a contemporary rendering of the Ten Commandments (see Exod. 20:1–17). State how you, your faith community, and/or your nation have followed and have violated the "commandments." Determine who benefits from following the commandments and who suffers when they are breached. Devise some specific strategies for following the commandments more closely. Determine the "rewards" for keeping the commandments.

- Find your denomination's faith creed or statement of faith. Identify the prophetic references it contains and determine how the denomination embodies its beliefs.

- Visit the website www.americanrhetoric.com, where you will find a selection of one hundred speeches. Select a speech and compare it with the concerns of a selected prophet. For instance, compare Amos with Dr. Martin L. King Jr.'s "I Have a Dream." Or, compare Habakkuk with Congressperson Shirley Chisholm's "For the Equal Rights Amendment." Or compare Micah with Cesar E. Chavez's "The Mexican-American and the Church." Or compare Jeremiah 1 with Barbara Jordan's "Democratic National Convention Keynote Address of 1976" alongside Franklin D. Roosevelt's "First Inaugural Address of 1933." Or compare Ezekiel 37 with Rev. Jesse Jackson's two Democratic National Convention addresses in 1984 and 1988. Or compare Jonah with Che Guevara's "Mobilizing the Masses for the Invasion." Or compare Isaiah 61 with Elie Wiesel's "The Perils of Indifference." The possibilities are endless and you may consider contemporary speeches by leaders and politicians in your own community or national setting. The aim is to see what issues the prophets raise that continue to have relevance today.

- Stage a courtroom scene placing a contemporary community leader, politician, or your faith community on trial or before a Senate hearing—for war crimes, for overstepping protocol, for breaching peace treaties, whatever contemporary issue you may want to address. Use what you know about the legal system and/or what you know from television shows, such as *The People's Court, Judge Judy*, and others.

- Sponsor a dinner honoring one of the prophets—it can be serious or a "roast"—and determine who will speak and what they will say.

- Write funeral services for one or more of the prophets— include music, readings, eulogy, obituary, pall bearers, and so on. Focus on the prophet's legacy.

- Create debates between or among the prophets—Isaiah and Habakkuk, Jeremiah and Micah, Joel and Ezekiel, Jeremiah and Jonah. Shake things up and have them engage in conversation about their messages, their passions, their strategies, their regrets, and their triumphs.

- Imagine one or more of the prophets in therapy. What kinds of concerns do the prophets raise? How do the therapists respond? Compose a series of questions and responses—use what you know about psychotherapy and popular "therapists" such as Dr. Joyce Brothers, Dr. Phil, and others.

PREACHING

Effective preaching requires study, reflection, and attention to public speaking. Remember that Jonah's sermon was brief yet massively effective. Each preacher brings her or his own methods of sermon development, and I encourage you to do what works for you. However, every preacher should start with the text itself by reading it! Use a good, reliable translation; I prefer the New Revised

Standard Version (NRSV). However, I always consult more than one translation and version—paying attention to differences in wording, ordering, punctuation, and so on. *The Jewish Study Bible*, edited by Adele Berlin and Marc Zvi Brettler (Oxford: Oxford University Press, 2004), is a solid resource for the prophets. Then, ask a series of questions of the text, including these:

- What is the text saying? What are the details?

- Who are the participants in the text? What is said about the participants—what can we know about them?

- Who speaks and what does she or he say?

- Who is silent? Why?

- What is the setting that has given rise to this particular text?

- What is happening in the text? Who acts and what does he or she do? What are the issues involved? How are the issues resolved?

- Who reacts in the text? How? Why?

- What happens before and after this particular text? How does this text fit into the larger text?

- Are there any other biblical texts that relate to this particular text? Where? Under what circumstances are there connections?

- What senses (sight, sound, smell, taste, etc.) are aroused by the text? What emotions are evoked?

- How can we connect to the text today?

- What is God doing in the text? Why? To what end does God act?

- What is believable in the text? What raises doubt?

- Who in the Bible will disagree with this particular text? What would that person say instead?

- Who in the church will disagree with this text? What would that individual say instead?

- How does this text fit into God's wider purposes for creation and humanity?

- What does the text say about our lives and world today?

- What does the text call us to be or to do? What prevents us from fulfilling the text's call? What will happen if we fail to heed the text's call? What will happen if we fulfill the text's call?

These and other questions can be asked before any other sources are consulted. This method helps the preacher to see the text before her or his opinions are colored by the opinions of others. Only after wrestling with questions like these is the preacher ready to move on to study aids. Now the preacher is ready to let the sermon unfold.

As you continue studying the Hebrew prophets, consider the following questions to shape your sermons:

- Where is God in a world filled with pain, suffering, anguish, and anxiety? What should we do to be co-creators of shalom with God?

- What should be our response when we feel that God has abandoned us?

- What is the relationship between religion and politics? How are we to deal with politics as people of God?

- How is it possible to find hope in even the most horrendous situations? Must we blame ourselves for how things turn out?

- How do we see and deal with an angry God? How does an angry God see and deal with us? How do we avoid blaming the victim?

- On what basis do we make ethical choices in our everyday lives? What could we improve in order to reflect God's values and intentions for creation?

- What does it mean to be "in" the world and not "of" the world?

- How are we to make sense of the anger and destruction we find in the prophetic literature?

- For people who are obsessed with feeling good, how do we understand that God is also Judge?

- How do we move to the other side of loss, failure, and grief? What is the role of faith?

- What does God say about the senseless violence of our day? Who is responsible for the violence? What can the people of God or the church do about the violence?

- How do we understand the image of God as warrior in our postmodern, postcolonial day?

- Can social change happen through revolution and/or violence?

- How do we worship in the midst of despair, anger, and hopelessness that accompany contemporary realities?

The reflection questions for each unit serve to stimulate some thinking about how these texts can be used in the church. I am sure that you have some creative ways of preaching and teaching these prophetic texts. I hope these suggested activities and themes will spark your imagination and unlock the stories so that they can bless us. The point to remember is that the texts focus on justice and community. A resource for understanding these texts includes liberation theologies that continue to emerge—there are liberation movements across the globe. Some movements are verbal and visible while others are subtle and underground. Activists and community organizers are finding new life and new allies in their efforts to create more equitable and sustainable communities. It is a good idea to seek out new avenues of justice work—and to find ways to support such efforts.

A Closing Word

The Bible is not just a sacred text—it is a blueprint for what life as children of God can be. We have not reached the destination; and the journey is a curvy, twisty route that is filled with detours, delays, construction sites, and dead ends. There are few rest stops and, just when we think we know where we are going, a roadblock impedes our progress. We are not to be dismayed by the obstacles; we are to embrace them and wait for the lessons they have to teach us about ourselves, about each other, and, ultimately, about God. From cover to cover, the Bible is about God: God's nature and passions, God's intentions for creation, and God's dealings with us.

Despite the signs of the times, or because of them, we are to focus on God and God's will and way. God loves us—even when God lets us deal with the consequences of our choices and decisions, even when we fashion death-dealing institutions and think we are secure; even when we are blind to our part in oppressing others; even when we are in denial about our sinful ways; even when we think we know what we really don't know—God seeks us to save and love us. And we are not saved just for ourselves, but rather for the whole of creation—that shalom should be the order of the day rather than the exception. God creates us—all of us—in the divine image and likeness. God expects us to live up to this high calling; certainly, the prophets challenge us to do better and to be better.

Sunday after Sunday, month after month, year after year, we hear the same story over and over again:

- The story of the prophets, who tell us that God is Redeemer *and* Judge; that we are responsible for our choices and decisions; that life is not always fair; that God is always hanging around somewhere—in exile, in our flight away from God, in the joyous return home from the wilderness—waiting for us to turn to God in gratitude and hope.

- The story of the psalmists, who set to music and poetry the raw reality of physical, mental, and spiritual exile; the hopelessness and frustration that threaten to overwhelm us; our lamentations about the conditions of the world too often because of our own hands and hearts; and even praise to God for our blessings and for lessons learned through pain.

- The story of the Gospel writers, who reassure us that God decisively shows grace and mercy through the birth, life, ministry, death, and resurrection of Jesus Christ, our brother and friend—even to those of us who wonder if we are worthy.

Through hard times and difficult stories that stretch the limits of our belief and faith in a loving and just God, in a God who is on the side of the oppressed, we are forced to consider our own faith. Can it be that God really does love us and wants to be connected to us? Can it be that despite all we do to push God away, there is still room for divine forgiveness and compassion?

We cannot cajole or coerce God to do our bidding. We cannot know how God will get our attention to challenge us, teach us, and keep us. There are no easy answers or magic formulas or simple steps to an easy life. We must struggle and wrestle with how we live our lives. While we are too much like the nations that surrounded our biblical ancestors, we still must make choices. The adventure in life is not that we always have the answers—the adventure is that answers are possible. In the tension between uncertainty and knowing lies the creative and infinite possibility that we might see something, feel something, taste something, discover something— something miraculous and wonderful, something meaningful and grace-filled, something that delivers us from death and despair.

The prophets help us because they are rooted in the teachings of the Torah and the choice is clear:

> [God says] ... See, I have set before you today life and prosperity, death and adversity. I call heaven and earth to witness against you today that I have set before you life and death, blessings and curses. Choose life so that you and your descendants may live.... (Deut. 30:15, 19b)

May we choose wisely ... or live the consequences, in God's love!

RESOURCES FOR FURTHER STUDY

ONLINE RESOURCES

For information about the prison industrial complex, go to Critical Resistance at http://criticalresist.live.radicaldesigns.org/, a site that is building an international movement to end "society's use of prisons and policing as an answer to social problems" and is part of the global struggle against inequality and powerlessness.

For information about the U.S. "war on terror," go to the Centre for Research on Globalization at www.globalresearch.ca, an independent research organization and media group of writers, scholars, journalists, and activists that publishes news articles, commentary, background research, and analysis on a broad range of issues, focusing on social, economic, strategic, and environmental processes.

For information on the plight of family farmers, go to the National Family Farm Coalition at http://www.nffc.net/, an organization that represents family farm and rural groups whose members face the deepening economic recession in rural communities and that works to maintain a sustainable, economically just, healthy, safe, and secure food and farm system.

For information on the military industrial complex, visit http://www.militaryindustrialcomplex.com/.

DVD RESOURCES

Bowling for Columbine, directed by Michael Moore (United Artists, 2002), deals with guns and violence.

Century of the Self, directed by Adam Curtis (BBC Four, 2002), is a BBC special that deals with the psychology of consumerism.

Eyes on the Prize: America's Civil Rights Years (1954–1965), a PBS documentary series directed by Henry Hampton (PBS Home Videos, 1987), chronicling the civil rights movement in the United States, became available on DVD April 2010.

A Lion in the House, a film directed by Steven Bognar and Julia Reichert (DOCUDRAMA, 2008), follows five families as they deal with the illness of a child and their interactions with the health care system.

The Overspent American: Why We Want What We Don't Need, a film produced by the Media Education Foundation (2006), deals with the "new consumerism" as set forth in a book of the same title by Juliet Schor (New York: Basic Books, 1998).

Sicko, a documentary directed by Michael Moore (WeinStein Co., 2007), deals with the health care system in the United States and around the globe.

Trouble the Water, an HBO documentary directed by Tia Lessin and Carl Deal (Zeitgeist Films, 2008), follows a couple, Kimberly and Scott Rivers Roberts, as they chronicle the aftermath of Hurricane Katrina in the Ninth Ward of New Orleans.

When the Levees Broke: A Requiem in Four Acts, a Spike Lee documentary (HBO, 2006), deals with the New Orleans tragedy after Hurricane Katrina.

Why We Fight, a film directed by Eugene Jarecki (Sony Picture Classics, 2005), deals with the U.S. military industrial complex.

PRINT RESOURCES

Bell, Derrick. *Ethical Ambition: Living a Life of Meaning and Worth.* New York: Bloomsbury, 2002.

Blenkinsopp, Joseph. *A History of Prophecy in Israel.* Louisville: Westminster John Knox Press, 1996.

———. *Sage, Priest, Prophet: Religious and Intellectual Leadership in Ancient Israel.* Louisville: Westminster John Knox Press, 1995.

Boadt, Lawrence, ed. *The Hebrew Prophets: Visionaries of the Ancient World.* New York: Palgrave Macmillan, 1997.

Bright, John. *A History of Israel.* Third ed. Philadelphia: Westminster Press, 1981.

Brueggemann, Walter. *An Introduction to the Old Testament: The Canon and Christian Imagination.* Louisville: Westminster John Knox Press, 2003.

———. *The Prophetic Imagination.* Second ed. Minneapolis: Augsburg Fortress, 2001.

Carroll, Robert P. *When Prophecy Failed: Reactions and Responses to Failure in the Old Testament Prophetic Traditions.* London: SCM Press, 1979.

Cary, Phillip. *Jonah: Theological Commentary on the Bible Series.* Grand Rapids, Mich.: Brazos Press, 2008.

Dufour, Jules. "The Worldwide Network of U.S. Military Bases: The Global Deployment of U.S. Military Personnel." Global Research, July 1, 2007, http://www.globalresearch.ca/index.php?context=va&aid=5564. Accessed April 12, 2009.

Essex, Barbara. *Misbehavin' Monarchs: Exploring Biblical Rulers of Questionable Character.* Cleveland: Pilgrim Press, 2006.

González, Justo L., and Catherine G. González. *Liberation Preaching: The Pulpit and the Oppressed.* Nashville: Abingdon Press, 1980.

Gottwald, Norman. *The Politics of Ancient Israel.* Louisville: Westminster John Knox Press, 2007.

Heller, Roy L. *Power, Politics, and Prophecy: The Character of Samuel and the Deuteronomistic Evaluation of Prophecy.* Library of Hebrew Bible/Old Testament Studies 440 (formerly Journal for the Study of the Old Testament Supplement Series). Ed. Claudia V. Camp and Andrew Mein. New York: T & T Clark, 2006.

Hiebert, Theodore. "The Book of Habakkuk: Introduction, Commentary, and Reflections." *New Interpreter's Bible.* Vol. 7, 623–55. Nashville: Abingdon Press, 1996.

Horsley, Richard A., ed. *In the Shadow of Empire: Reclaiming the Bible as a History of Faithful Resistance.* Louisville: Westminster John Knox Press, 2008.

Johnson, Chalmers. "America's Empire of Bases." Published January 15, 2004 by TomDispatch.com and found on CommonDreams Newscenter, http://www.commondreams.org/views04/0115-08 .htm. Accessed April 12, 2009.

Miller, Patrick D. "The Book of Jeremiah: Introduction, Commentary, and Reflections." *New Interpreter's Bible.* Vol. 6, 553–926. Nashville: Abingdon Press, 2001.

Quinn-Miscall, Peter D. *Reading Isaiah: Poetry and Vision.* Louisville: Westminster John Knox Press, 2001.

Schor, Juliet B. *The Overspent American: Why We Want What We Don't Need.* New York: Harper Paperbacks, 1999.

Seitz, Christopher R. "The Book of Isaiah 40–66: Introduction, Commentary, and Reflections." *New Interpreter's Bible.* Vol. 6, 307–552. Nashville: Abingdon Press, 2001.

Sharp, Carolyn J. *Old Testament Prophets for Today.* Louisville: Westminster John Knox Press, 2009.

Shipler, David K. *The Working Poor: Invisible in America.* New York: Vintage Books, 2005.

Trible, Phyllis. "The Book of Jonah: Introduction, Commentary, and Reflections." *New Interpreter's Bible.* Vol. 7, 463–529. Nashville: Abingdon Press, 1996.

————. *Rhetorical Criticism: Context, Method, and the Book of Jonah.* Minneapolis: Fortress Press, 1994.

Tucker, Gene M. "The Book of Isaiah 1–39: Introduction, Commentary, and Reflections." *New Interpreter's Bible.* Vol. 6, 25–305. Nashville: Abingdon Press, 2001.

OTHER BOOKS FROM THE PILGRIM PRESS
BY BESTSELLING AUTHOR BARBARA J. ESSEX

BAD GIRLS OF THE BIBLE
The Sequel

978-0-8298-1824-6/paper/128 pp/$16.00

Several years ago, Essex launched the bestselling Bible study *Bad Girls of the Bible: Exploring Women of Questionable Virtue*. It has become a favorite of teachers and preachers everywhere, with Bible study groups, sermon series, retreat themes, and seminary classes forming across the country to learn from it and the Bible. Now Essex has returned with a command performance focusing on fourteen new stories of biblical women from the Hebrew Bible and New Testament.

BAD GIRLS OF THE BIBLE
Exploring Women of Questionable Virtue

0-8298-1339-X/paper/114 pages/$14.00

Designed as a fourteen-week study, this resource explores biblical accounts of traditionally misunderstood or despised women as they are presented in the Bible. Reflection questions are included along with suggestions for preaching and teaching.

BAD BOYS OF THE BIBLE
Exploring Men of Questionable Virtue

0-8298-1466-3/paper/124/$16.00

Cain, Abraham, Adam, Samson, Lot, Jacob, and Jepthah are well-known men of the Bible who were strong and faithful, yet also weak and challenged. In this bestselling text, Essex takes readers on a journey to explore male giants of faith.

BAD BOYS OF THE NEW TESTAMENT
Exploring Men of Questionable Virtue

0-8298-1672-0/paper/128 pp./$16.00

Bad Boys of the New Testament, a seven-week small group study session, is part of Essex's popular series of Bible studies. Each study unit reviews the stories of selected biblical "bad boys" in the New Testament, such as the elder brother of the Prodigal Son parable, Pharisees, Judas Iscariot, Pontius Pilate, and Ananias.

KRAZY KINFOLK

Exploring Dysfunctional Families in the Bible

0-8298-1654-2/paper/128 pp/$16.00

In *Krazy Kinfolk*, Essex's user-friendly book, she continues in the tradition of her popular series of Bible studies. Each study unit reviews the stories of selected biblical "dysfunctional" families, such as Abraham, Sarah, and Hagar; Jacob, Leah, and Rachel; Moses, Miriam, and Aaron; Lois, Eunice, and Timothy; Mordecai and Esther; and Mary, Martha, and Lazarus. After each text is reviewed, a historical explanation is offered to help make the story come alive in an understandable way. Reflection questions close each study and can be used personally or in groups.

MISBEHAVIN' MONARCHS

Exploring Biblical Kings of Questionable Character

978-0-8298-1655-6/paper/128 pp/$16.00

In this popular Bible study series, Essex examines the lives and leadership of some renowned biblical monarchs and lesser known kings—their style of leadership, the women in their lives, which prophets were prominent during their reigns, and what the Bible says (and does not say) about war. Monarchs examined include Saul, David, Solomon, Rehoboam, Samuel, Jeroboam, and Hoshea, among others.

To order these or any other books from The Pilgrim Press, call or write to:

THE PILGRIM PRESS
700 PROSPECT AVENUE EAST
CLEVELAND, OHIO 44115-1100

PHONE ORDERS: 1-800-537-3394 • FAX ORDERS: 216-736-2206
Please include shipping charges of $6.00 for the first book and $1.00 for each additional book.

Or order from our web sites at www.pilgrimpress.com and www.ucpress.com.

Prices subject to change without notice.